No Gallbladder Diet Cookbook

Discover the Path to Digestive Harmony with Nutrient-Rich, Easy-to-Prepare Dishes that Will Keep You Nourished, Satisfied, and Thriving

By Marge Myles

Table Of Contents

Chapter 1: Understanding Your Diet Post-Gallbladder Removal

Embarking on a journey through life without a gallbladder presents a unique set of challenges and opportunities, especially when it comes to your diet. This transition requires not just a change in what you eat, but a deeper understanding of how your body now processes food. The absence of the gallbladder, an organ once responsible for storing bile and aiding in fat digestion, necessitates a thoughtful approach to your meals to maintain comfort and health. It's about finding harmony in your digestive system through the foods you choose to nourish your body with.

Adjusting your diet post-gallbladder removal is not merely about restrictions; it's an invitation to rediscover food in a way that supports your body's new needs. This means embracing a diet rich in key nutrients that facilitate digestion and absorption without the gallbladder's bile reservoir. Healthy fats, soluble fiber, lean proteins, and a variety of vitamins and minerals become central to your dietary choices, ensuring that each meal contributes to your overall well-being.

This new dietary landscape is not one you have to navigate alone. Equipped with knowledge and guided by a spirit of curiosity, you can transform your diet into one that not only meets your nutritional needs but also brings joy and satisfaction to your dining table. It's an opportunity to explore new flavors, textures, and cooking techniques, all while keeping your digestive health in mind.

As you move forward, remember that adjusting to life without a gallbladder is a personal journey. It involves listening to your body, experimenting with foods, and finding what works best for you. With patience, persistence, and a positive outlook, you can craft a diet that not only suits your post-gallbladder life but enhances it, allowing you to thrive and enjoy food in ways you never thought possible.

1.1 The Role of the Gallbladder in Digestion

Embarking on a journey through the digestive system reveals a fascinating world where each organ plays a pivotal role in turning the food we eat into the fuel that powers our lives. Among these vital players, the gallbladder might seem unassuming, yet it performs a critical function that affects not just how we process fats but also how we absorb essential nutrients.

This understanding is particularly important for individuals who are navigating life without this small, but significant, organ.

The gallbladder's primary role in our digestive ballet involves the storage and release of bile, a substance produced by the liver that is essential for breaking down and absorbing fats. Bile acts much like a detergent, emulsifying fats in the digestive tract, which allows enzymes to work more effectively in breaking them down into absorbable molecules. This process is not only crucial for the utilization of fats but also for the absorption of fat-soluble vitamins, which are vital for our overall health.

However, the removal of the gallbladder necessitates a shift in this delicate dance. Without the gallbladder's reservoir, bile flows directly from the liver into the small intestine in a continuous, but less concentrated, stream. This alteration requires those affected to reconsider their approach to eating, particularly concerning fat intake, to maintain comfort and health.

Understanding the gallbladder's role offers a foundation for those without this organ to adapt successfully. It prompts a reassessment of dietary habits and opens up an opportunity to explore new foods and methods of preparation that are both nutritious and supportive of digestive health. Through this lens, the absence of the gallbladder becomes not just a challenge to overcome but a catalyst for developing a deeper connection with the food we eat and a more nuanced appreciation for the body's ability to adapt and thrive.

The Gallbladder's Role

In the intricate dance of digestion, where every organ contributes its unique steps, the gallbladder plays a critical yet often underappreciated role. This small, pear-shaped organ, nestled quietly under the liver, is a key player in the digestive process, specifically in the management and breakdown of fats. Its job, while singular, is mighty, impacting not just how we digest fats but also how we absorb essential nutrients and maintain overall digestive health.

The gallbladder's primary function revolves around bile, a vital digestive fluid produced by the liver. Bile's composition, rich in bile acids, cholesterol, and bilirubin, equips it uniquely for breaking down and absorbing fats. When we consume foods containing fats, they are initially processed in the stomach and then proceed to the small intestine, where the majority of digestion and absorption takes place. It's here that bile enters the scene, introduced into the digestive tract from the gallbladder in response to signals that fats are present.

Upon detecting fats, the small intestine releases cholecystokinin (CCK), a hormone that acts as a green light for the gallbladder to contract and squirt stored bile into the intestine. This action is not merely a response but a critical intervention. Bile salts emulsify fats, breaking them down into tiny droplets that increase their surface area. This transformation is crucial because it allows lipase, a digestive enzyme, to work more efficiently, breaking these fats down into fatty acids and glycerol that can be absorbed into the bloodstream and utilized by the body.

But the gallbladder's influence extends beyond fats. Bile also facilitates the absorption of fat-soluble vitamins (A, D, E, and K), which are crucial for various bodily functions, including vision, blood clotting, and maintaining healthy skin and bones. Moreover, bile helps in the excretion of waste products from the body, including excess cholesterol and bilirubin, a byproduct of red blood cell breakdown. Thus, the gallbladder, though small, plays a multi-faceted role in maintaining our health, from ensuring we can utilize the energy in fats to helping keep our blood clean and our bones strong.

The story of the gallbladder is one of efficiency and precision. By storing bile and releasing it in concentrated bursts, the gallbladder ensures that the body has ready access to this critical digestive agent precisely when needed. This process exemplifies the body's ability to regulate its internal processes tightly, ensuring that digestion proceeds smoothly and efficiently.

Understanding the gallbladder's role in digestion illuminates the challenges faced by those who undergo cholecystectomy, the surgical removal of the gallbladder. Without this reservoir for bile, the continuous drip of bile from the liver into the intestine can lead to a mismatch between the availability of bile and the presence of dietary fats, necessitating adjustments in diet and lifestyle to maintain digestive health and comfort.

In exploring the gallbladder's role, we gain not only a deeper appreciation for this small organ but also a clearer understanding of the complexities of digestion. This knowledge forms the foundation for adapting to life without a gallbladder, guiding dietary choices, and fostering a lifestyle that supports digestive health and overall well-being. The journey post-gallbladder removal is one of adaptation and discovery, requiring a nuanced approach to diet and an awareness of the body's needs. Armed with knowledge and understanding, individuals can navigate this path with confidence, embracing a diet that supports their health and enables them to thrive.

Life Without a Gallbladder

Navigating the journey of life after the removal of the gallbladder presents a unique set of challenges and adjustments, particularly when it comes to the realm of digestion and dietary habits. The absence of this small but significant organ means the body must adapt to a new normal in processing and digesting fats, a task the gallbladder once played a pivotal role in. This adaptation is not insurmountable but requires a thoughtful approach to food and an understanding of how the body now handles dietary fats without the gallbladder's bile storage capacity.

With the gallbladder's removal, the direct storage for bile is no longer present, altering the way bile enters the digestive system. The liver continues its production of bile, vital for breaking down fats, but without the gallbladder, bile is released directly into the small intestine at a constant, slow rate, regardless of food intake. This change can lead to difficulties when consuming meals high in fat, as there may not be enough bile available at one time to adequately emulsify large amounts of fat, leading to potential digestive discomfort and changes in bowel habits.

This new digestive landscape post-gallbladder removal necessitates a dietary adjustment to manage and mitigate the potential side effects. It involves a more mindful approach to eating, particularly with regard to fat intake. Emphasizing smaller, more frequent meals can help manage the steady flow of bile into the small intestine, making it easier for the body to digest fats more efficiently and minimize digestive discomfort. This approach also underscores the importance of the types of fats consumed; prioritizing healthy fats that are easier to digest, such as those from avocados, nuts, and fish, can make a significant difference in comfort and nutritional absorption.

Moreover, the adjustment to life without a gallbladder extends beyond just managing fat intake. It encompasses a holistic approach to eating and nutrition, where the quality of the diet as a whole plays a crucial role in maintaining digestive health and overall well-being. Incorporating a wide variety of nutrient-dense foods, rich in vitamins, minerals, and fiber, supports the digestive system and ensures the body receives the essential nutrients it needs. This dietary strategy not only helps in managing the direct effects of gallbladder removal but also contributes to a healthy, balanced lifestyle.

The transition to this new way of eating and living does not happen overnight and can vary significantly from person to person. Listening to one's body becomes paramount, as individual responses to different foods and dietary patterns can provide valuable cues for adjusting and refining one's diet. This personalized approach allows for the discovery of what works best for each individual, fostering a diet that supports digestion, minimizes discomfort, and enhances overall health.

In essence, the absence of the gallbladder opens up a path to a deeper understanding of one's dietary needs and how best to support the body's adjusted digestive processes. It's an opportunity to embrace healthier eating habits, explore new foods and recipes, and learn how to nourish the body in a way that promotes digestive harmony and well-being. With the right knowledge and adjustments, living without a gallbladder can lead to a fulfilling and healthy life, where food continues to be a source of pleasure and nutrition.

Adjusting Your Diet

Embarking on a dietary adjustment journey following gallbladder removal is an essential step towards ensuring continued digestive health and overall well-being. This process is not merely about limiting or eliminating certain foods; it's a comprehensive approach to redefining one's relationship with food, understanding its impact on the body, and discovering how to enjoy a balanced, nutritious diet that caters to a changed digestive system.

The absence of the gallbladder necessitates a more nuanced approach to consuming fats. While the body can still digest fats, the mechanism by which bile is delivered to the digestive tract changes. Without the gallbladder's storage capability, bile from the liver trickles continuously into the small intestine, which can be less efficient at breaking down large amounts of fats consumed in a single meal. Therefore, one of the first steps in adjusting your diet is to moderate fat intake, focusing on the quality rather than merely the quantity of fats. Incorporating smaller amounts of healthy fats, such as those found in avocados, olive oil, and fatty fish, throughout the day can help ensure that these fats are digested more effectively, reducing the likelihood of discomfort.

However, adjusting your diet goes beyond simply managing fat intake. It involves a holistic reevaluation of eating habits to support digestion and enhance nutrient absorption. Emphasizing a diet rich in fruits, vegetables, whole grains, and lean proteins can provide the body with essential nutrients while easing the digestive process. These foods are not only easier to digest but also contribute to a feeling of fullness and satisfaction without overburdening the digestive system.

Moreover, the timing and size of meals play a significant role in adapting to life without a gallbladder. Opting for smaller, more frequent meals can prevent the digestive system from becoming overwhelmed and can aid in the more efficient use of bile. This eating pattern helps in managing energy levels throughout the day and supports steady digestion, minimizing potential issues such as bloating, gas, or discomfort.

In addition to what and how you eat, paying attention to the way you eat is equally important. Mindful eating practices, such as chewing food thoroughly and eating in a relaxed setting, can significantly improve the digestive process. These practices encourage a slower pace of eating, allowing for better digestion and absorption of nutrients, and ensuring that the digestive system is not unduly stressed.

The journey of dietary adjustment is deeply personal, and what works for one individual may not work for another. It's crucial to listen to your body and observe how it responds to different foods and eating patterns. Keeping a food diary can be an invaluable tool in this process, allowing you to track your meals, note any digestive discomfort, and adjust your diet accordingly. Over time, this practice can help you develop a personalized eating plan that supports your health and suits your lifestyle.

Adapting your diet after gallbladder removal is an opportunity to embrace a healthier way of eating that not only caters to your digestive system's needs but also enhances your overall health. With careful consideration and a willingness to experiment and learn, you can create a diet that is not only nourishing and balanced but also enjoyable and satisfying. This approach to eating, grounded in understanding and mindfulness, is the key to thriving without a gallbladder and living a full, vibrant life.

A New Relationship with Food

Embarking on life without a gallbladder presents an opportunity to redefine one's relationship with food, transforming it from a source of potential discomfort into a journey of discovery and nourishment. This transition is not merely about managing dietary restrictions; it's about embracing a new perspective on eating that prioritizes well-being, balance, and joy in every meal. The absence of the gallbladder necessitates a closer examination of how foods affect the body, offering a unique chance to cultivate a diet that supports optimal health while still delighting the palate.

This new relationship with food goes beyond simple substitutions or eliminations; it invites a holistic approach to nutrition, where mindful eating becomes a practice of listening to and respecting the body's signals. It's about understanding that without the gallbladder's bile storage, the body requires a more nuanced approach to digesting fats. This understanding paves the way for selecting foods that are not only delicious but also beneficial for digestion and overall health.

Adapting one's diet post-gallbladder removal involves a thoughtful consideration of fat intake, focusing on incorporating healthy fats in moderation. These fats, found in foods like avocados, nuts, seeds, and oily fish, are essential for absorbing fat-soluble vitamins and providing the body with energy. The emphasis shifts towards preparing meals that are both nutritious and gentle on the digestive system, exploring cooking methods such as steaming, baking, and grilling, which retain flavor without adding excessive fat.

Moreover, this new dietary approach encourages the exploration of a wide variety of fruits, vegetables, whole grains, and lean proteins, diversifying the diet to ensure it is rich in all the nutrients the body needs to thrive. Experimenting with herbs, spices, and new cooking techniques can make meals exciting and flavorful, challenging the misconception that a diet suited for post-gallbladder life is bland or restrictive.

In embracing a new relationship with food, meal planning and preparation become key elements of success. Taking the time to plan meals ensures that the diet remains balanced and varied, reducing the temptation to reach for convenience foods that may not be as compatible with post-gallbladder removal dietary needs. Learning to prepare meals in advance can also alleviate the stress of cooking, making it easier to maintain healthy eating habits despite a busy schedule.

This journey also opens the door to learning more about nutrition and how different foods affect the body, fostering a sense of empowerment and control over one's health. It's an opportunity to become more attuned to the body's needs, recognizing which foods enhance well-being and which to approach with caution. Through trial and error, individuals can develop a personalized diet that supports their digestive health without sacrificing flavor or enjoyment.

Ultimately, developing a new relationship with food after gallbladder removal is about more than just adapting to dietary changes; it's about embracing a lifestyle that prioritizes health, well-being, and the joy of eating. It's a chance to rediscover the pleasures of food, exploring new tastes and textures, and celebrating the nourishment that food provides. With each meal, individuals can celebrate their resilience and their body's ability to adapt, finding new ways to enjoy food that are both satisfying and supportive of their health.

1.2 Adjusting to Life Without a Gallbladder

Embarking on a journey without a gallbladder presents a unique set of challenges and opportunities for anyone who has undergone cholecystectomy. This significant change in your digestive system calls for a thoughtful reassessment of your dietary habits and lifestyle choices. As you step into this new phase, it's crucial to understand that your body's ability to process certain foods—especially fats—has been altered. Without the gallbladder's bile reservoir, the continuous, direct flow of bile into your intestines can affect digestion and necessitate adjustments to your eating patterns.

This transition is not just about subtraction—eliminating or severely limiting certain foods from your diet. It's about addition and adaptation, discovering new foods and cooking methods that support your digestive health while keeping your meals enjoyable and varied. The focus is on nurturing your body with nutrient-rich foods that are easy to digest, promoting a balanced intake of healthy fats, soluble fiber, lean proteins, and a wide array of vitamins and minerals.

The path to adjusting to life without a gallbladder is as much about mental and emotional adaptation as it is about physical changes. It requires cultivating a mindset of patience and resilience, understanding that finding the right dietary balance for your unique body may take time. Through trial and observation, you'll learn to identify which foods and eating habits work best for you, leading to fewer digestive issues and a more comfortable and satisfying eating experience.

Moreover, this journey underscores the importance of listening to your body's cues and being proactive about your health. It invites you to become an active participant in your well-being, armed with knowledge and a willingness to experiment. By embracing this new way of life with optimism and creativity, you can find a fulfilling path forward, one that not only addresses the challenges of living without a gallbladder but also opens up new possibilities for enjoying food and maintaining a healthy, vibrant lifestyle.

Embracing Healthy Fats

In the journey of adjusting to life without a gallbladder, the nuanced approach to incorporating fats into your diet becomes crucial. The body still requires fats for numerous vital functions, including hormone production, cell structure maintenance, and the absorption of fat-soluble vitamins. However, the key lies not in the elimination of fats but in choosing the right kinds and understanding how to introduce them into your diet in a way that harmonizes with your body's new digestive process.

Healthy fats, such as monounsaturated and polyunsaturated fats found in avocados, olive oil, nuts, seeds, and fatty fish like salmon and mackerel, should be the cornerstone of your fat intake. These fats not only contribute to heart health by lowering bad cholesterol levels but also play a role in reducing inflammation throughout the body, which can be particularly beneficial during the post-surgery healing process.

However, the shift to healthy fats requires more than just selecting the right types; it demands attention to how these fats are consumed. The absence of the gallbladder means bile is released into the small intestine in a constant trickle rather than in response to fat intake, which can make digesting large amounts of fat at once challenging. To navigate this, integrating healthy fats in smaller, more measured amounts throughout the day can help ensure that they are digested more efficiently. This approach allows the liver to manage the bile flow more effectively, aligning with the body's adjusted capacity to process fats.

Moreover, embracing healthy fats is not just about the physical health benefits; it's also about enjoying the flavors and textures that make meals satisfying and enjoyable. By carefully selecting and moderating healthy fats, you can create a diet that supports your digestive health while still delighting in the culinary pleasures that fats bring to the table. This balanced approach to fats is not only a testament to the resilience of the body but also to the adaptability of the palate, allowing for a diet that is as nourishing as it is enjoyable.

Mindful Eating

Adapting to a life without a gallbladder necessitates a more conscious and deliberate approach to eating, which is where the concept of mindful eating plays a pivotal role. This practice transcends the simple act of choosing healthier foods and delves into how we eat, focusing on the pace, the awareness, and the enjoyment of each meal. It's about creating a connection between the food on our plate and our body's needs, recognizing that how we eat can significantly impact our digestive health and overall well-being.

Mindful eating involves paying close attention to the flavors, textures, and sensations of food, savoring each bite, and listening to the body's hunger and fullness cues. This attentiveness not only enhances the dining experience but also allows for better digestion. By eating slowly and chewing thoroughly, we facilitate the breakdown of food, making it easier for the body to digest and absorb nutrients, especially in the absence of the gallbladder. This methodical approach to eating can also prevent overeating, which is particularly beneficial when the body's capacity to digest fats efficiently is compromised.

Moreover, mindful eating encourages a deeper appreciation for food, fostering a healthier relationship with eating that transcends nutritional value alone. It invites individuals to engage with their meals in a way that supports physical health while also providing psychological satisfaction.

In the context of post-gallbladder removal, where dietary adjustments are necessary, mindful eating becomes an invaluable tool. It empowers individuals to navigate their new dietary landscape with confidence, ensuring that each meal supports their digestive system while still bringing joy and fulfillment.

In essence, mindful eating is not just a dietary adjustment but a lifestyle change that enhances the way we interact with food. It's a practice that supports the body's adjusted digestive process, promoting better health and a more enjoyable eating experience. By embracing mindful eating, individuals can navigate the challenges of life without a gallbladder with grace, ensuring that their diet remains both nourishing and pleasurable.

Diversifying Your Diet

Embracing a diverse diet is a cornerstone of nutritional wellness, especially after the removal of the gallbladder. This concept goes beyond merely adding an array of colors to your plate; it's about enriching your diet with a wide variety of nutrients that support your body's new way of processing food. Incorporating a broad spectrum of fruits, vegetables, whole grains, lean proteins, and healthy fats ensures that your body receives the essential vitamins, minerals, and other nutrients it needs to function optimally.

A diversified diet plays a pivotal role in maintaining balanced digestion and overall health post-gallbladder removal. Each food group brings its unique benefits: fruits and vegetables are rich in dietary fiber, which aids in digestion and helps regulate bowel movements; whole grains provide sustained energy and further digestive support; lean proteins are essential for tissue repair and growth; and healthy fats contribute to satiety and the absorption of fat-soluble vitamins.

Moreover, diversifying your diet can help mitigate some of the digestive challenges that may arise after gallbladder surgery. By ensuring a balance of soluble and insoluble fiber, for example, you can help manage bile flow and reduce symptoms like bloating or discomfort. Additionally, exploring different food groups and ingredients can also lead to the discovery of foods that agree with your body and those that don't, allowing for more personalized and effective dietary adjustments.

However, diversifying your diet is not just about physical health; it's also about enjoyment and satisfaction. Discovering new foods and flavors can make meals more enjoyable, turning the necessity of dietary adjustment into an opportunity for culinary exploration.

It encourages creativity in the kitchen and can make eating a more engaging and pleasurable experience, even within the dietary constraints post-gallbladder removal.

In essence, a diversified diet is a fundamental strategy for navigating life without a gallbladder. It supports the body's adjusted digestive needs, promotes optimal health, and turns each meal into an opportunity for nourishment and discovery. By embracing variety in your diet, you can ensure that your meals are not only balanced and beneficial but also enjoyable and satisfying.

Hydration and Fiber

In the post-gallbladder removal diet, the twin pillars of hydration and fiber take on an even more significant role. This combined strategy not only supports the body's adjusted digestive process but also enhances overall health and well-being. The removal of the gallbladder necessitates a careful balance in the diet, where adequate fluid intake and the right types of fiber become crucial for maintaining digestive comfort and efficiency.

Hydration, the act of ensuring the body receives ample fluids, is foundational to good health. In the context of digestive health, especially after gallbladder removal, it aids in the smooth passage of food through the intestines, helping to prevent constipation—a common concern for many in this situation. Water, the simplest yet most effective hydrant, supports the body's ability to process and absorb nutrients efficiently and plays a vital role in the elimination of waste. Consuming sufficient water throughout the day keeps the digestive system fluid and responsive, minimizing potential discomforts such as bloating and constipation.

Fiber, particularly soluble fiber, acts in concert with hydration to optimize digestion. Found in foods like oats, apples, berries, and legumes, soluble fiber absorbs water, forming a gel-like substance that helps to bind bile acids and slow down the digestion process. This slower transit time can be particularly beneficial for individuals without a gallbladder, as it allows for a more gradual absorption of fats and nutrients, reducing the likelihood of digestive upset. Furthermore, fiber-rich foods add bulk to the stool, facilitating a more regular bowel movement pattern and contributing to the overall health of the digestive tract.

Incorporating a diet rich in both hydration and fiber post-gallbladder removal is not just about addressing specific digestive concerns; it's about embracing a holistic approach to health that recognizes the interconnectivity of the body's systems.

By focusing on these elements, individuals can support their digestive health, enhance nutrient absorption, and ensure their diet is as comfortable as it is nutritious. This approach underscores the importance of not just what we eat but how we support our body's processes through our dietary choices, leading to a more balanced and healthful lifestyle.

Listening to Your Body

Adjusting to life after gallbladder removal entails more than simply altering the foods you eat; it involves a holistic reevaluation of your diet and how your body processes food. This period of adjustment offers a unique opportunity to explore your nutritional landscape anew, prioritizing the integration of key nutrients that support your digestive system's altered functionality. Emphasizing the importance of healthy fats, soluble fiber, lean proteins, and a wide array of vitamins and minerals is crucial. These elements serve as the pillars of your new diet, each playing a vital role in ensuring your meals are not only nourishing but also enjoyable.

Without the gallbladder's bile storage, your body requires fats that are easier to digest in smaller quantities. Avocados, nuts, seeds, and fish rich in monounsaturated and polyunsaturated fats should become staples in your diet, aiding in heart health and digestion. The significance of soluble fiber escalates, as it helps regulate digestion by absorbing excess bile. Incorporating foods like oats, apples, and legumes into your diet can mitigate discomfort such as bloating.

Lean proteins become indispensable, providing essential nutrients without overburdening your digestive system. Options like poultry, omega-3-rich fish, and plant-based proteins ensure your meals remain balanced. Attention to vitamins and minerals, particularly those that are fat-soluble, becomes paramount due to altered absorption rates post-surgery. A diet rich in leafy greens, sweet potatoes, and fortified dairy products can help fill any nutritional gaps.

Hydration also plays a key role in supporting digestive health, with water, herbal teas, and other non-caffeinated beverages maintaining fluid balance and aiding nutrient absorption. The journey towards dietary adaptation is deeply personal, requiring patience, experimentation, and a willingness to listen to your body's cues. This exploration is not solely about identifying what to eat but how to enjoy food in a way that celebrates nutrition, connection, and the pleasure of eating. Creating a supportive network, whether through family, friends, or professionals, can provide encouragement and guidance tailored to your needs. Understanding and integrating key nutrients into your diet is essential for maintaining both digestive health and overall well-being. This transition is not merely a series of adjustments but a profound opportunity to foster a deeper connection with your body, embracing change with optimism and creativity. By focusing on balance, nutrition, and enjoyment, you can lay the foundation for a diet that supports your digestive system and enhances your quality of life.

Experimentation and Patience

In the journey of adapting to life without a gallbladder, embracing the principles of experimentation and patience is essential. This transition is not merely about following a prescribed set of nutritional guidelines but about embarking on a deeply personal exploration of how your body responds to different foods and portions. The absence of the gallbladder necessitates a more nuanced approach to eating, one that is attuned to the body's altered digestive process.

Experimentation plays a pivotal role in this new dietary landscape. It involves a willingness to try a variety of foods, observing how your body reacts to each. This process is crucial, as it helps identify which foods enhance your digestive well-being and which ones to avoid. It's about finding the right balance that works for your unique digestive system, which may no longer handle certain fats and fibers as it once did. Through trial and error, you can discover a diet that not only meets your nutritional needs but also brings joy and satisfaction to your meals.

Patience is equally important in this journey. Adjusting to a gallbladder-free diet doesn't happen overnight. It requires time and patience as you slowly introduce new foods and observe their impact. This gradual approach helps mitigate digestive discomfort and allows your body to adapt to its new normal. It's about giving yourself grace and space to learn and grow in your understanding of what works best for you.

Furthermore, this process of experimentation and patience encourages a deeper connection with your body. It invites you to listen closely to its signals, understanding that each person's experience post-gallbladder removal is unique. Embracing this approach means recognizing that setbacks and successes are part of the journey, and both provide valuable insights into creating a diet that supports your health and happiness.

As you navigate this path, remember that this is a journey of discovery. It's an opportunity to get creative with your meals, exploring new recipes and ingredients that cater to your adjusted dietary needs. This exploration is not just about avoiding discomfort but about enriching your life with a variety of nutritious and delicious foods that nourish both body and soul. Through experimentation and patience, you can build a fulfilling and balanced diet that fosters digestive harmony and overall well-being, turning the challenge of living without a gallbladder into an opportunity for dietary and personal growth.

The cornerstone of this new dietary framework includes a focus on healthy fats, lean proteins, soluble fiber, and a broad spectrum of vitamins and minerals, each playing a unique and vital role in your overall well-being.

Healthy fats become paramount, as they are essential for heart health and can be more readily digested. Sources such as avocados, nuts, and seeds, along with fish rich in omega-3 fatty acids, should be staples in your meals. These fats not only provide the necessary energy but also support your body's healing process, all while ensuring that you're not overwhelming your system with difficult-to-digest fats.

Lean proteins are crucial for maintaining muscle health and overall energy levels. Given the digestive system's adjusted capabilities, incorporating lean meats like poultry and fish, as well as plant-based proteins such as beans and lentils, can provide the necessary nutrients without taxing your system.

Soluble fiber stands out for its role in helping to regulate the digestive process, particularly in managing bile flow without the gallbladder's storage capacity. Foods rich in soluble fiber, like oats, apples, and carrots, become key in promoting a smooth digestive experience, helping to mitigate potential discomforts such as bloating.

Vitamins and minerals, especially those that are fat-soluble, warrant special attention to ensure your body receives the nutrients it needs to function optimally. A colorful variety of fruits and vegetables, alongside fortified foods, can help cover these nutritional bases, supporting everything from bone health to immune function.

Hydration also plays a crucial role in this new dietary equation. Proper fluid intake is essential for facilitating digestion and helping to absorb nutrients effectively, making water, herbal teas, and other hydrating beverages fundamental components of your daily intake.

As you embrace this foundational shift in your dietary habits, remember that it's about more than just adhering to a list of do's and don'ts. It's about creating a balanced, enjoyable approach to eating that supports your health without sacrificing the pleasure of food. This holistic perspective on nutrition is not just about managing life without a gallbladder; it's about thriving in spite of it, armed with the knowledge and tools to navigate your dietary journey with confidence and joy.

Integrating Key Nutrients into Your Meals

Weaving the essential nutrients into your daily meals is an art that requires both creativity and mindfulness, especially after gallbladder removal. This endeavor goes beyond simply understanding which nutrients are beneficial; it's about crafting meals that are both nourishing and delightful, ensuring that your diet remains varied and enjoyable. To achieve this, focus on incorporating a balanced mix of healthy fats, lean proteins, soluble fiber, vitamins, and minerals into every meal, creating a tapestry of flavors and textures that cater to your body's adjusted digestive capabilities.

Start your day with a breakfast that energizes and supports your digestive health. Consider a smoothie that blends fruits high in soluble fiber, like berries or bananas, with leafy greens for vitamins and a scoop of protein powder or Greek yogurt for protein. This combination ensures a nutrient-rich start with the added benefit of hydration.

For lunch and dinner, aim for a harmony of flavors and nutrients. A plate featuring a lean protein source, complemented by a side of fibrous vegetables and a whole grain or legume, offers a balanced meal that supports your dietary needs. Grilled chicken or fish, paired with quinoa and roasted vegetables, can provide the perfect mix of nutrients to keep your digestive system running smoothly.

Snacking should also be approached with the same level of thoughtfulness. Opt for snacks that deliver a good mix of soluble fiber, healthy fats, and protein. Almond butter on whole-grain toast or a serving of Greek yogurt with fresh fruit are excellent choices that satisfy hunger and provide essential nutrients.

Integrating key nutrients into your meals is not just about dietary requirements; it's an opportunity to explore new culinary horizons. Experiment with different ingredients and cooking methods to discover what works best for you. This process is not only beneficial for your physical health but also enriches your culinary experience, making every meal a chance to nourish your body and delight your palate.

As you adapt to your new dietary landscape, remember that variety is the spice of life. Embrace the diversity of foods within your nutritional needs, creating meals that are as satisfying to your taste buds as they are beneficial to your health. This balanced approach to eating ensures that your journey without a gallbladder is not only manageable but enjoyable, filled with delicious opportunities to support your well-being.

The Role of Supplements

Navigating the dietary changes after gallbladder removal often leads to the realization that while a well-balanced diet is crucial, it may not always be sufficient to meet all your nutritional needs. This is where supplements can play a pivotal role, acting as a bridge to fill any nutritional gaps that your adjusted diet might leave. However, the decision to incorporate supplements should be approached with discernment and, ideally, under the guidance of a healthcare professional.

Supplements can be particularly beneficial in ensuring you receive an adequate intake of fat-soluble vitamins (A, D, E, and K), which your body might struggle to absorb efficiently in the absence of a gallbladder. Since these vitamins are essential for a range of bodily functions, from maintaining healthy vision to supporting your immune system, their supplementation can be vital for maintaining your overall health.

Omega-3 fatty acids, often found in fish oil supplements, are another key nutrient that might require supplementation. Known for their anti-inflammatory properties and their role in heart health, omega-3s can be harder to absorb without a gallbladder. Supplementing with fish oil can ensure you're getting these important fats, even if your body's ability to digest fat has been compromised.

Probiotics also deserve a special mention, as they can help manage the balance of good bacteria in your gut, supporting digestion and potentially easing some of the gastrointestinal symptoms associated with gallbladder removal.

It's important to remember that supplements are just that—supplementary. They are meant to enhance a diet that is already as balanced and nutritious as possible, not replace it. Furthermore, not all supplements are created equal, and their quality can vary significantly. Seeking advice from a healthcare provider can help you choose the right supplements to complement your diet, ensuring they align with your specific nutritional needs and health goals.

Incorporating supplements into your post-gallbladder removal diet, when done thoughtfully and under professional guidance, can be a strategic move towards optimizing your digestive health and overall well-being. This approach allows you to tailor your nutritional intake more precisely, ensuring that your body receives the support it needs to thrive in its new state.

The Joy of Eating

Rediscovering the joy of eating in the aftermath of gallbladder removal is an essential component of your journey towards health and well-being. This process involves not just adapting your diet to meet new digestive needs but also embracing the pleasure and satisfaction that food can bring. It's a reminder that food is not merely fuel but a source of enjoyment, connection, and exploration.

Transitioning to a gallbladder-free diet might initially seem daunting, with concerns about dietary restrictions overshadowing the pleasure of eating. However, this change offers a unique opportunity to explore a wide array of foods and flavors that not only comply with your dietary needs but also delight your taste buds. It's about finding new favorites among the array of suitable foods and discovering creative ways to prepare them that keep meals interesting and enjoyable.

Moreover, this journey reinforces the importance of mindful eating—savoring each bite and appreciating the flavors and textures of your food. Mindfulness enhances the dining experience, making meals more satisfying and helping you tune into your body's cues, which is especially important when adjusting to life without a gallbladder.

Sharing meals with family and friends adds another layer of joy to eating. Food has the power to bring people together, creating moments of connection and shared pleasure. These social interactions can make meals more gratifying, providing a sense of normalcy and belonging as you navigate your dietary changes.

Ultimately, the joy of eating post-gallbladder removal lies in the balance between nourishing your body and satisfying your soul. It's an invitation to celebrate food, to experiment with new ingredients and recipes, and to find happiness in the kitchen and at the dining table. Embracing this approach can transform your dietary adjustments into a positive and enriching experience, reminding you that even without a gallbladder, eating can still be one of life's great pleasures.

As we wrap up our initial exploration into adapting your diet after gallbladder removal, it's clear that this journey is as much about nurturing your body as it is about embracing change with optimism and creativity. The transition to a gallbladder-free life is not just a series of dietary adjustments but a profound opportunity to connect with your body on a deeper level, understanding its needs and responding with care and intention.

The key insights we've discussed pave the way for a dietary approach that prioritizes balance, nutrition, and enjoyment. By focusing on healthy fats, incorporating soluble fiber, choosing lean proteins, and ensuring a rich intake of essential vitamins and minerals, you lay the foundation for a diet that supports your digestive system and overall health. This holistic approach not only addresses the physical adjustments your body undergoes in the absence of the gallbladder but also attends to your well-being and satisfaction at the dining table.

Embracing this new way of eating requires patience, experimentation, and an open mind. Each step forward is an opportunity to learn more about what works best for your unique body and lifestyle. It's a journey that encourages you to explore new foods, experiment with different recipes, and find joy in the kitchen again, all while keeping your health at the forefront.

As you continue on your path, remember that the goal is not just to manage your diet without a gallbladder but to thrive. This chapter lays the groundwork for a fulfilling dietary life post-gallbladder removal, offering insights and strategies to help you navigate this transition with confidence. Armed with knowledge and empowered by your own experiences, you're well-equipped to create a nourishing, enjoyable, and balanced diet that supports your journey toward digestive harmony and overall well-being.

Chapter 2: Essential Diet Tips for Living Without a Gallbladder

Embarking on life without a gallbladder presents a unique set of challenges, especially when it comes to your diet. This change necessitates a nuanced approach to eating, one that balances your nutritional needs with the goal of minimizing digestive discomfort. It's a journey that requires not just adaptation but also an opportunity to rediscover the joy of eating through a new lens. The key lies in understanding how the absence of the gallbladder affects digestion, particularly the digestion of fats, and adjusting your diet to accommodate this change.

This section aims to guide you through the essentials of crafting a diet that supports your body post-surgery. You'll learn the importance of selecting foods that harmonize with your altered digestive process and discover strategies to incorporate these foods into your daily life. From managing fat intake to identifying foods that soothe and nourish, the goal is to equip you with the knowledge and tools needed to create a balanced, varied diet.

Moreover, we'll explore the significance of meal timing and portion sizes, emphasizing how small, frequent meals can facilitate easier digestion and enhance overall well-being. Mindful eating practices will be highlighted, encouraging you to eat slowly and with intention, fostering a deeper connection with your food and how it makes you feel.

Navigating dietary changes without a gallbladder is not about imposing strict limitations but about finding what works best for your body. It's about making informed choices that promote digestive health without sacrificing the pleasure and satisfaction derived from eating. Through a combination of practical advice and empathetic guidance, this chapter aims to support you on your journey to dietary adjustment, ensuring that each meal brings you closer to achieving digestive harmony and a joyful culinary experience.

2.1 Managing Fat Intake: What You Need to Know

Adjusting to life without a gallbladder necessitates a thoughtful reevaluation of how you approach your diet, particularly when it comes to managing fat intake. This challenge, while daunting at first, offers a unique opportunity to deepen your understanding of nutrition and its impact on your health. It's about embarking on a journey that not only accommodates your body's new way of digesting fats but also enriches your overall dietary experience.

The essence of managing fat intake post-gallbladder removal lies in recognizing the different types of fats and their effects on your body. This knowledge is pivotal in making informed choices that support your digestive health without compromising the pleasure of eating. The goal is to foster a diet that balances the need for essential fatty acids and fat-soluble vitamins with the body's adjusted capacity to process fats. This balance is crucial for maintaining your well-being and ensuring that your meals are both nourishing and enjoyable.

Embracing this new dietary approach requires patience, experimentation, and a willingness to learn. It's about gradually introducing healthy fats into your diet, paying close attention to portion sizes, and being mindful of how your body responds. This process is not just about limiting certain foods; it's a comprehensive strategy that includes choosing cooking methods that minimize added fats while enhancing natural flavors, and incorporating a variety of nutrient-dense foods that support your overall health.

This chapter aims to guide you through the intricacies of managing fat intake, offering insights and strategies to navigate this aspect of your diet confidently. By understanding the role of fats, learning how to select and prepare foods in a way that aligns with your body's needs, and discovering how to enjoy a rich and varied diet, you can achieve a sense of dietary harmony and well-being that supports your lifestyle post-gallbladder removal.

Understanding Fat Digestion

Navigating your dietary needs after gallbladder removal demands a nuanced understanding of how your body processes fats. Without the gallbladder, the dynamic of fat digestion undergoes a significant transformation, affecting how you should approach your diet to maintain optimal health and comfort. This adjustment period is not merely about reducing fat intake; it's about comprehensively understanding the types of fats and how they interact with your altered digestive system.

The gallbladder's primary role in digestion involves storing bile produced by the liver and releasing it into the small intestine to emulsify fats, making them easier to digest. In its absence, bile drips directly into the intestine at a constant but slower rate, which can make the digestion of large amounts of fat at one time more challenging. This doesn't mean all fats are off-limits; rather, it emphasizes the importance of choosing the right types of fats and consuming them in moderation.

Healthy fats, particularly monounsaturated and polyunsaturated fats, should be the focal point of your fat intake. These fats, found in avocados, olive oil, nuts, and fatty fish, can still be digested without a gallbladder and offer numerous health benefits, including supporting heart health and reducing inflammation. Incorporating these into your diet in small, regular amounts can help your body adjust to the absence of a gallbladder while still absorbing the essential fatty acids and fat-soluble vitamins your body needs.

It's also crucial to understand the impact of different types of fats on your digestive system. Saturated fats, commonly found in red meat and processed foods, can be harder to digest and may lead to discomfort. Being mindful of the quantity and types of fats you consume can make a significant difference in how you feel after meals.

Adapting to this new way of managing fat intake requires patience and attentiveness to your body's cues. By focusing on healthy fats, moderating portions, and listening to how your body responds, you can craft a diet that supports your digestive health and overall well-being without the gallbladder. This approach to understanding fat digestion is not just about making dietary adjustments; it's about embracing a lifestyle that promotes nourishment, balance, and enjoyment in every meal.

Healthy Fats: A New Best Friend

In the journey of adjusting to life without a gallbladder, it's crucial to redefine your relationship with fats. The concept of "healthy fats" becomes central to this new dietary narrative, transforming them from a component to be wary of into your new best friends. These fats, rich in monounsaturated and polyunsaturated fatty acids, are not only more digestible for those without a gallbladder but also bring a host of health benefits that can enhance your diet and overall well-being.

Monounsaturated fats, found in olive oil, avocados, and certain nuts, are known for their ability to support heart health and regulate blood sugar levels. Similarly, polyunsaturated fats, which include omega-3 and omega-6 fatty acids found in fish, flaxseeds, and walnuts, play a crucial role in brain function and cellular health. Incorporating these fats into your diet in moderation can help ensure that your body receives the essential fatty acids it needs without overwhelming your digestive system.

Transitioning to a diet that emphasizes these healthier fats doesn't just support your digestive health; it also opens up a world of culinary possibilities. Avocado can be a creamy addition to smoothies or salads, while a drizzle of high-quality olive oil can elevate a simple dish. Nuts and seeds make for nutrient-dense snacks or garnishes, adding texture and flavor to meals. Even fatty fish, like salmon, can be a weekly staple, providing both protein and omega-3 fatty acids.

Adapting to this shift means not just adding these foods to your diet but also learning to appreciate the subtle ways they enhance your meals. It's about embracing a holistic approach to eating that sees fats not as foes but as allies in your quest for a balanced, nourishing diet. By making healthy fats your new best friend, you embark on a path that prioritizes both your digestive comfort and your taste buds, proving that a life without a gallbladder can still be rich in flavor and health benefits.

Portion Control and Meal Timing

Mastering the art of portion control and strategic meal timing becomes a cornerstone of dietary management after gallbladder removal. This nuanced approach to eating is not just about what you eat but also how and when you eat it, ensuring that your body can comfortably digest meals without the gallbladder's bile storage capability. By adopting a mindful approach to portion sizes and the timing of your meals, you create an environment that supports your digestive system, allowing it to process foods more efficiently and with less discomfort.

Portion control is essential, as smaller, more manageable meal sizes can prevent the overwhelming of your digestive system, which is now continuously receiving a slow drip of bile rather than the concentrated bursts that helped digest larger amounts of fat. Eating smaller portions more frequently throughout the day can help maintain a steady flow of nutrients without putting too much pressure on your digestion at any one time.

Similarly, meal timing plays a crucial role in optimizing your digestive health. Establishing a regular eating schedule helps your body adapt to a consistent digestive routine, reducing the likelihood of digestive distress. It's particularly beneficial to avoid eating large meals late at night when your body's digestive processes slow down, as this can lead to discomfort and disruptions in your sleep pattern.

Integrating mindful eating practices, such as chewing food thoroughly and eating without distraction, further enhances the effectiveness of portion control and meal timing. These habits encourage a slower pace of eating, allowing for better digestion and absorption of nutrients, and enabling you to tune into your body's hunger and fullness cues more accurately.

Embracing portion control and mindful meal timing is not merely a dietary adjustment but a lifestyle change that fosters a harmonious relationship with food. This approach not only minimizes digestive issues post-gallbladder removal but also contributes to a more mindful, enjoyable eating experience. By focusing on how you eat just as much as what you eat, you lay the foundation for a nourishing diet that supports your health and well-being in the absence of your gallbladder.

Cooking Techniques That Make a Difference

In the culinary journey of adapting to life without a gallbladder, the methods you choose to cook your food can significantly influence your digestive well-being. Understanding and employing cooking techniques that minimize fat content while maximizing flavor and nutritional value becomes crucial. This approach is not just about avoiding certain cooking methods; it's a creative exploration of how to prepare your meals in a way that supports your health and satisfies your palate.

Steaming, grilling, baking, and poaching are techniques that stand out for their ability to cook foods thoroughly without the need for excessive fats. Steaming vegetables, for example, preserves their crunch and color while maintaining their nutrient content, making them a delightful side to any meal. Grilling can impart a smoky flavor to meats and vegetables alike, offering a tantalizing taste experience without the added fat of frying. Baking and poaching are similarly gentle on the digestive system, allowing for the preparation of tender, flavorful dishes that are both satisfying and easy to digest.

These cooking methods not only cater to the needs of those without a gallbladder but also open up a spectrum of culinary possibilities. By experimenting with herbs, spices, and marinades, you can elevate the natural flavors of your ingredients, turning a simple piece of fish or a selection of vegetables into a mouthwatering masterpiece. It's an invitation to get creative in the kitchen, discovering new recipes and techniques that enrich your diet without compromising on taste or health.

Embracing these cooking techniques marks a significant step in adjusting to your new dietary needs. It's about making conscious choices in how you prepare your meals, ensuring they nourish your body and delight your senses. This approach to cooking is not just a dietary adjustment; it's a lifestyle change that celebrates the joy of eating well, offering a path to digestive harmony and culinary enjoyment.

Incorporating Fat-Soluble Vitamins

Adjusting to life without a gallbladder necessitates a thoughtful approach to incorporating fat-soluble vitamins into your diet. Vitamins A, D, E, and K are essential for a multitude of bodily functions, from maintaining vision and bone health to supporting the immune system and blood clotting. However, the absorption of these vitamins becomes more challenging without the gallbladder's bile storage, making it crucial to find ways to ensure your body still receives these vital nutrients.

Incorporating fat-soluble vitamins into your diet doesn't just mean focusing on the foods that are rich in these nutrients; it's also about understanding how to consume them in a way that enhances absorption. This includes pairing vitamin-rich foods with healthy fats to aid in their assimilation. For example, a salad dressed with olive oil can enhance the absorption of vitamin K from leafy greens, while a serving of salmon provides both vitamin D and omega-3 fatty acids, facilitating a synergistic absorption process.

Diversifying your diet to include a wide range of sources for these vitamins is equally important. Brightly colored vegetables and fruits are excellent sources of vitamin A, while fortified foods can provide vitamin D during the winter months when sunlight exposure is limited. Nuts and seeds are rich in vitamin E, and leafy greens are a great source of vitamin K. By incorporating a variety of these foods into your meals, you can ensure a balanced intake of fat-soluble vitamins, supporting your overall health and well-being.

It's also worth considering that while dietary adjustments are vital, supplementation may be necessary for some individuals to meet their nutritional needs fully. Consulting with a healthcare professional can provide personalized advice on how to manage your vitamin intake effectively, ensuring that your post-gallbladder removal diet supports your health in the best way possible.

This approach to incorporating fat-soluble vitamins into your diet reflects a broader understanding of nutrition and health. It's not just about what you eat but how you combine and consume your foods to support your body's needs, especially in the absence of a gallbladder.

By being mindful of these considerations, you can navigate your dietary adjustments with confidence, ensuring that you continue to thrive and enjoy a vibrant, healthy life.

The Role of Fiber

Understanding the role of fiber in your diet, especially after gallbladder removal, is pivotal for maintaining digestive health and overall well-being. Fiber, particularly soluble fiber, plays a crucial role in managing the body's use of fats and aiding in the normalization of bowel movements. For individuals without a gallbladder, incorporating the right amount of fiber is essential for facilitating the digestion process and helping to absorb the continuous flow of bile into the intestines.

Soluble fiber, found in foods such as oats, apples, carrots, and legumes, has the unique ability to dissolve in water, forming a gel-like substance that can help regulate the body's digestion of fats and slow down the overall digestion process. This slower digestion is beneficial for those without a gallbladder, as it allows for a more gradual absorption of fats and nutrients, reducing the likelihood of digestive discomfort.

Incorporating fiber into your diet also offers the benefit of improving cholesterol levels and controlling blood sugar, contributing to a reduced risk of developing heart disease and diabetes. Beyond its direct health benefits, a high-fiber diet can also make meals more satisfying, helping to control appetite and support weight management efforts.

However, it's important to increase fiber intake gradually to allow your digestive system to adjust without causing discomfort. Drinking plenty of water is also crucial when increasing fiber, as it helps to move fiber through the digestive system more easily, preventing constipation and promoting a healthy gut.

Exploring a variety of fiber-rich foods and finding enjoyable ways to include them in your meals can make managing your diet without a gallbladder not only easier but also more enjoyable. Whether it's starting the day with a bowl of oatmeal, enjoying a crisp apple as a snack, or incorporating lentils into your dinner, the right fiber choices can support your digestive health and enhance your overall diet quality.

Staying Hydrated

Maintaining adequate hydration is a cornerstone of health for everyone, but it becomes even more critical after gallbladder removal. Water is essential for facilitating digestion, aiding in the absorption of nutrients, and ensuring the smooth operation of your body's natural processes. For those adjusting to life without a gallbladder, staying well-hydrated helps manage the continuous flow of bile into the intestines, preventing potential issues such as bile salt diarrhea, which can occur when bile is not adequately absorbed.

Hydration plays a multifaceted role in your health. Beyond its direct impact on digestion, adequate water intake supports overall bodily functions, including maintaining body temperature, lubricating joints, and flushing toxins from your system. It can also improve your skin's appearance and boost energy levels, contributing to a sense of well-being.

The importance of hydration extends to how it can influence your eating habits. Often, feelings of hunger can be mistaken for dehydration. By drinking sufficient water, you may find it easier to distinguish between true hunger and thirst, aiding in weight management and preventing overeating. Water can also be a valuable tool for managing appetite, as it contributes to a feeling of fullness, which can help control portion sizes.

Incorporating a variety of hydrating fluids beyond water, such as herbal teas and broth-based soups, can add diversity to your fluid intake while supporting hydration. However, it's essential to be mindful of beverages that can dehydrate, such as those containing caffeine or alcohol, and balance your intake accordingly.

Ensuring you drink enough water throughout the day requires conscious effort, especially in the beginning. Carrying a water bottle, setting reminders, and including water-rich foods in your diet, like fruits and vegetables, can all help meet your hydration needs. Embracing these habits not only supports your digestive health post-gallbladder removal but also enhances your overall health and vitality, proving that something as simple as drinking water can have profound effects on your well-being.

The Joy of Eating

Rediscovering the joy of eating is a vital part of adapting to life without a gallbladder. This journey isn't merely about adhering to dietary restrictions; it's an opportunity to explore new flavors, textures, and culinary experiences that not only nourish your body but also delight your senses. The process of adjusting your diet can often feel overwhelming, but it opens up a new realm of possibilities for creativity and enjoyment in your meals.

Eating should be a pleasurable experience, one that brings satisfaction and joy. With the right approach, you can craft meals that are both compatible with your digestive needs and rich in the flavors and textures you love. This involves experimenting with a wide range of ingredients, from fresh fruits and vegetables to lean proteins and healthy fats, discovering how to combine them in ways that are both delicious and supportive of your health.

The joy of eating extends beyond the food itself. It encompasses the entire experience of meal preparation, from selecting ingredients to cooking and sharing meals with loved ones. There's a certain satisfaction in learning new cooking techniques, trying out healthy recipes, and tweaking them to suit your taste preferences and nutritional requirements. This process can transform mealtime from a routine task into an enjoyable and rewarding part of your day.

Moreover, embracing this new way of eating encourages a mindful approach to meals, where you savor each bite and appreciate the nourishment it provides. It's about finding balance, allowing yourself to enjoy your favorite foods in moderation while focusing on the rich variety of nutrients that support your digestive health.

Ultimately, the joy of eating after gallbladder removal is about embracing a positive and open mindset toward food and nutrition. It's an invitation to celebrate the diverse array of foods available, experimenting with new dishes, and finding pleasure in the act of eating well. By focusing on the opportunities this change presents, you can enjoy a fulfilling dietary life that enhances your health and happiness.

2.2 Foods to Embrace and Avoid

Embarking on a journey of dietary transformation after gallbladder removal is a pivotal step toward reclaiming your digestive health and overall well-being. This phase of your journey requires not just an understanding of the body's changed nutritional needs but also a mindful approach to embracing and avoiding certain foods.

The essence of this guidance lies in harmonizing your diet with your body's new digestive capabilities, focusing on foods that nourish and support you while steering clear of those that may lead to discomfort or digestive issues. It's about creating a balanced, enjoyable diet that caters to your unique needs without feeling restrictive. Through mindful selection and preparation of foods, you can enjoy a wide array of meals that are not only delicious but also conducive to your health. This chapter aims to provide you with the knowledge and tools necessary to navigate these dietary adjustments with confidence, ensuring that each meal brings you closer to digestive harmony and enhanced quality of life.

Foods to Embrace

Embracing the right foods after gallbladder removal is crucial for maintaining digestive health and ensuring that your diet remains balanced and satisfying. The focus should be on selecting foods that your body can easily process without the gallbladder's aid in fat digestion. Lean proteins, including poultry, fish, and plant-based options like lentils and tofu, are excellent choices. They provide essential amino acids without the high fat content that can be harder to digest post-surgery. Whole grains, such as quinoa, brown rice, and oats, are also beneficial. They offer the fiber needed for healthy digestion and help keep you satiated, reducing the urge for less healthy snacks.

Low-fat dairy alternatives are preferable, as high-fat dairy products might lead to discomfort. Almond milk, coconut yogurt, and low-fat cheeses can be good substitutes, offering the calcium and protein your body needs without the digestive challenges. Fruits and vegetables are pillars of a healthy diet, especially important in the absence of a gallbladder. They supply vital vitamins and minerals, along with fiber to aid digestion. However, it's important to introduce high-fiber foods gradually to allow your digestive system to adjust.

Healthy fats are still necessary for your diet. Sources like avocados, nuts, seeds, and olive oil can provide the fats your body needs without overwhelming your system. These fats are crucial for absorbing fat-soluble vitamins and supporting overall health. In integrating these foods into your diet, creativity and variety are key. Experiment with different grains, try new fruits and vegetables, and explore plant-based proteins. The goal is not just to avoid digestive discomfort but to enjoy a rich and diverse diet that keeps you both nourished and satisfied.

Listening to your body and how it reacts to different foods will be your guide. Some may find they can handle small amounts of foods traditionally advised against, while others might need to be more cautious. The journey is highly personal and requires patience, experimentation, and a willingness to adapt. By focusing on foods that support your digestive health, you're taking a significant step towards a balanced and joyful dietary life post-gallbladder removal.

Foods to Avoid

Navigating your diet after gallbladder removal involves not only embracing certain foods but also recognizing those that might be best to limit or avoid. Without the gallbladder's bile reservoir, digesting high-fat and heavily processed foods can become more challenging, potentially leading to discomfort.

This adjustment doesn't mean your meals will be bland or unenjoyable; rather, it's an opportunity to explore a variety of foods that agree with your body while maintaining a rich and balanced diet. High-fat foods, particularly those rich in saturated fats like certain cuts of meat, full-fat dairy products, and fried foods, can be more difficult for your body to digest. These foods may lead to discomfort or digestive issues, such as bloating and indigestion. Similarly, processed and fast foods, often high in unhealthy fats, sugars, and additives, can disrupt your digestive health and contribute to an unbalanced diet. It's beneficial to shift focus toward whole, nutrient-dense foods that support your digestive system and overall health.

Moreover, some vegetables and legumes, despite their nutritional benefits, can cause gas and bloating in sensitive individuals. It might be helpful to introduce these foods gradually and in moderation, paying attention to how your body reacts. Spicy foods and those with strong flavors might also pose a challenge for some, potentially irritating the digestive tract.

Caffeine and alcohol are other substances to approach with caution. They can stimulate the digestive system, possibly leading to discomfort. While moderation is key, you might find that reducing or eliminating these from your diet helps maintain digestive comfort.

Understanding the foods to limit or avoid is a crucial step in managing your diet post-gallbladder removal. However, it's equally important to listen to your body and recognize that individual reactions can vary. This journey is deeply personal, and what might be problematic for one person could be tolerable for another.

Keeping a food diary can be a valuable tool in identifying which foods work best for you, allowing you to craft a diet that is not only healthy and balanced but also enjoyable and satisfying. Embracing this adaptive approach to eating will help you navigate your dietary needs with confidence and ease.

Navigating Your Diet with Mindfulness

Adopting a mindful approach to your diet after gallbladder removal is about much more than just choosing the right foods; it's about fostering a deep connection between your mind and body. This holistic view encourages you to be fully present during meals, paying close attention to the tastes, textures, and effects of food on your body. Mindfulness in eating involves slowing down to savor each bite, which can lead to better digestion and an increased awareness of satiety cues, reducing the likelihood of overeating.

Moreover, this attentive approach extends to how you select and prepare your meals, encouraging a thoughtful consideration of ingredients and their preparation methods to ensure they align with your body's needs. It's about listening to your body's reactions to different foods and adjusting your diet accordingly, recognizing that your dietary needs may evolve over time.

Being mindful about your diet means also recognizing and respecting your body's new limits and capabilities without judgment. It's about embracing flexibility and patience, understanding that some days might be more challenging than others, and that's perfectly okay. This journey is not just about avoiding certain foods but about celebrating the vast array of foods that you can enjoy, discovering new flavors, and experimenting with new recipes that nourish and satisfy.

In essence, navigating your diet with mindfulness is a practice of self-care. It involves making choices that honor your health and well-being, cultivating gratitude for the nourishment you provide to your body, and finding joy in the simple pleasure of eating. By adopting a mindful approach to your diet, you're not just managing your digestive health post-gallbladder removal; you're taking steps towards a more balanced, healthful, and fulfilling lifestyle.

Practical Tips for Incorporating Foods to Embrace

Incorporating beneficial foods into your diet after gallbladder removal is a vital step towards maintaining a healthy and balanced lifestyle. This process involves a conscious effort to include foods that support your digestive health and provide the necessary nutrients without causing discomfort. One effective strategy is to plan your meals around these beneficial foods, ensuring that you have a variety of options that meet your dietary needs. This planning not only helps in avoiding foods that might trigger discomfort but also in discovering new and enjoyable ways to prepare and consume healthy meals.

Experimenting with different preparation methods can also make a significant difference in how your body processes these foods. For instance, steaming or baking instead of frying can retain the nutritional value of foods while making them easier to digest. Additionally, integrating a wide range of fruits, vegetables, lean proteins, and whole grains into your meals can enhance their flavor and nutritional content, making your diet both enjoyable and diverse.

Listening to your body is crucial; it will guide you in identifying which foods work best for you. Keeping a food journal can be an invaluable tool in this process, allowing you to track your reactions to different foods and adjust your diet accordingly. Over time, this mindful approach to incorporating beneficial foods will not only improve your digestive health but also enrich your overall well-being, making each meal a step towards a healthier, more vibrant life.

Navigating Foods to Avoid with Grace

Handling the foods that may not agree with you post-gallbladder removal requires a blend of awareness, adaptation, and a touch of creativity. It's about gracefully navigating your dietary landscape, identifying which foods might lead to discomfort, and finding satisfying alternatives that won't compromise your digestive health or culinary enjoyment. This journey is less about restriction and more about transformation, seeing the need to avoid certain foods not as a limitation but as an opportunity to explore a wider variety of ingredients and flavors.

Embracing this approach means becoming an investigator in your dietary world, paying close attention to how different foods affect you and being willing to adjust as needed. It involves learning to substitute ingredients in your favorite dishes with those that are more conducive to your new dietary needs, ensuring you can still enjoy the essence of what you love without the negative consequences.

Moreover, it's about cultivating a positive mindset towards your dietary choices, focusing on the abundance of foods you can enjoy rather than those you should avoid. This perspective shift can make a substantial difference in your overall satisfaction and success with your diet. By navigating your food choices with grace and intention, you embark on a path that not only supports your digestive health but also enriches your life with new tastes, textures, and experiences.

2.3 Eating Strategies to Minimize Discomfort

Navigating the dietary landscape after gallbladder removal requires thoughtful strategies to minimize discomfort and enhance digestive well-being. This part of the journey is about understanding and implementing eating practices that work in harmony with the body's modified digestive system. It involves a holistic approach that not only focuses on what to eat but also on how and when to eat, ensuring that every meal supports digestive health.

The key to this approach lies in adopting habits that ease the workload on the digestive system. By carefully selecting foods that are easier to digest and spacing meals throughout the day, individuals can help their body to efficiently process nutrients without overwhelming the digestive tract. Moreover, paying attention to the body's cues and adopting mindful eating practices can significantly enhance one's relationship with food, turning mealtime into a nurturing experience rather than a source of anxiety.

Furthermore, understanding the importance of balancing macronutrients and incorporating a variety of fiber-rich foods can aid in achieving a smoother digestive process. It's also essential to recognize the role of hydration in digestion, ensuring that fluid intake is adequate to support the body's needs.

This section aims to equip readers with practical, easy-to-implement strategies that are grounded in nutritional science and tailored to the unique needs of those without a gallbladder. By embracing these eating strategies, individuals can look forward to minimized digestive discomfort and an improved quality of life, marking a significant step towards digestive harmony and overall health.

Understanding Your Body's New Rhythms

After gallbladder removal, adapting to your body's new rhythms is essential for maintaining digestive health and overall well-being. This adjustment is not just about changing what you eat but also about recognizing and aligning with your body's altered digestive process. Without the gallbladder to store and concentrate bile, the liver now continuously releases bile directly into the intestines. This constant drip can impact how you digest fats, necessitating a more mindful approach to eating.

Understanding this new rhythm means acknowledging that your digestive system operates differently. It requires a shift in eating patterns to smaller, more frequent meals, which can help manage the bile's continuous flow and aid in the digestion of fats more effectively. This approach not only prevents overwhelming your digestive system but also supports steady energy levels throughout the day.

Moreover, tuning into your body's signals becomes crucial. Paying attention to how different foods affect you, noticing any signs of discomfort, and adjusting your diet accordingly can help you navigate this new terrain with greater ease. It's about developing a partnership with your body, where you listen and respond to its needs with care and consideration.

Embracing your body's new rhythms also involves embracing a journey of discovery—one where you learn to harmonize your dietary choices with your body's capabilities. It's a process that encourages patience, experimentation, and mindfulness, offering an opportunity to deepen your understanding of your health and to find joy in nourishing yourself in ways that support your digestive health and overall vitality.

Smaller, More Frequent Meals

Adopting a dietary pattern that includes smaller, more frequent meals can be particularly beneficial for individuals without a gallbladder. This approach helps in managing the digestive process more effectively, given the absence of a gallbladder's bile storage function. Without the gallbladder, the liver continues to produce bile, but the bile flows directly into the intestine, sometimes causing difficulty in digesting large amounts of fat at once. By eating smaller portions throughout the day, the body can better utilize the constant flow of bile, aiding in the digestion of fats more efficiently and reducing the risk of discomfort or digestive issues.

Furthermore, this eating strategy can contribute to more stable energy levels and better blood sugar control. Large meals can cause significant fluctuations in blood sugar levels, leading to spikes and crashes that affect energy and mood. Smaller, more frequent meals can help in maintaining a more consistent blood sugar level, providing steady energy throughout the day. This is especially important for individuals looking to maintain optimal health and well-being after gallbladder removal.

In addition to aiding digestion and stabilizing energy levels, this dietary adjustment can support weight management. Smaller, more frequent meals can prevent extreme hunger, reduce the likelihood of overeating, and help maintain a healthy metabolism. It's important to focus on nutrient-dense foods that provide the body with the vitamins, minerals, and other nutrients it needs to function at its best.

To implement this approach, consider planning meals and snacks that include a balance of carbohydrates, proteins, and healthy fats. This balance is crucial for satisfying hunger and providing the body with a well-rounded intake of nutrients. Incorporating a variety of fruits, vegetables, whole grains, lean proteins, and healthy fats into these smaller meals will ensure that the diet remains both nutritious and enjoyable.

It's also beneficial to pay attention to the body's hunger and fullness cues, eating when slightly hungry and stopping when comfortably full. This mindful eating practice can enhance the body's natural digestion and satisfaction from food, promoting a healthier relationship with eating.

Overall, transitioning to smaller, more frequent meals can offer numerous health benefits for those without a gallbladder. By facilitating better digestion, supporting stable energy levels, and aiding in weight management, this eating pattern can be a key component of a healthy lifestyle post-gallbladder removal. With thoughtful planning and mindful eating, individuals can enjoy a diverse and satisfying diet that supports their digestive health and overall well-being.

Mindful Eating Practices

Embracing mindful eating practices is about cultivating an awareness of the eating experience, focusing on the present moment, and listening to the body's cues regarding hunger and satiety. This approach encourages individuals to pay close attention to the flavors, textures, and aromas of their food, which can enhance the overall enjoyment of meals and help in recognizing when they are full, thus preventing overeating.

For those without a gallbladder, mindful eating is particularly beneficial as it aids in better digestion by encouraging slower eating, which allows for more effective use of bile in the digestion of fats.

Moreover, by being fully present during meals, individuals can identify specific foods that might trigger discomfort or digestive issues, enabling them to adjust their diets accordingly for better health outcomes. Mindful eating also involves making conscious food choices that support health and well-being, focusing on nutrient-dense foods that provide energy and sustenance without overwhelming the digestive system.

Implementing mindful eating can begin with simple steps, such as eating without distractions, chewing food thoroughly, and taking pauses during meals to assess hunger and fullness levels. This practice not only improves physical health by promoting better digestion and weight management but also enhances emotional well-being by reducing stress and improving one's relationship with food.

Over time, mindful eating practices can transform the act of eating from a routine task into a nourishing, enjoyable experience that supports both physical and emotional health. For those navigating life without a gallbladder, adopting these practices can be especially empowering, offering a pathway to improved digestion and a more satisfying dietary journey. By embracing mindfulness at mealtimes, individuals can achieve a deeper connection with their food and their bodies, leading to a more harmonious and healthful way of living.

Balancing Fats Wisely

Crafting a balanced approach to consuming fats is essential, particularly after gallbladder removal. This process requires a nuanced understanding of how different types of fats interact with the body, especially in the absence of the gallbladder's bile storage capability. The liver still produces bile, but it is directly released into the intestine, making the digestion of large amounts of fat at once more challenging. To adapt, incorporating a mix of healthy fats into the diet is key. These include monounsaturated and polyunsaturated fats found in avocados, nuts, seeds, and oily fish, which support heart health and reduce inflammation.

However, it's also critical to moderate the intake of saturated fats, commonly found in red meat and full-fat dairy products, as these can be harder to digest and may contribute to heart disease. Completely avoiding trans fats, present in many processed foods, is advisable, as they offer no nutritional benefit and pose significant health risks.

Understanding the role of omega-3 fatty acids is also important. These fats, particularly abundant in fish like salmon and sardines, are beneficial for their anti-inflammatory properties and support overall health. Incorporating these into meals several times a week can help in maintaining a balanced diet.

Portion control plays a pivotal role in balancing fats wisely. Even when consuming healthy fats, it's important to be mindful of serving sizes, as fats are calorie-dense. Using methods such as measuring oils with teaspoons rather than pouring directly from the bottle can help manage intake.

Moreover, cooking methods can influence the healthfulness of fats. Opting for baking, grilling, steaming, or sautéing over frying not only preserves the integrity of the healthy fats but also minimizes the addition of unhealthy fats during cooking.

Lastly, listening to the body's signals can guide individuals in how best to balance fats in their diet. Some may find they can tolerate a slightly higher intake of certain fats, while others may need to be more cautious. Regular check-ins with a healthcare provider can help tailor dietary choices to individual health needs and goals.

Adopting a balanced approach to fats is not just about reducing intake but about making informed choices that support digestive health and overall well-being. Through mindful selection and moderation of fats, individuals without a gallbladder can enjoy a rich and varied diet that supports their health and lifestyle.

Tailoring Fiber Intake

Customizing fiber intake is crucial for individuals navigating life without a gallbladder. This strategy is not merely about increasing fiber consumption; it's about finding the right balance that supports digestive health without causing discomfort. Fiber plays a key role in digestion, helping to regulate bowel movements and support a healthy gut microbiome. However, after gallbladder removal, the body's ability to digest high-fiber foods can change, making it essential to adjust fiber intake gradually.

Starting with soluble fiber found in foods like oats, apples, and flaxseeds can be beneficial, as it absorbs water and forms a gel-like substance, easing the digestion process. Soluble fiber can help manage diarrhea by slowing down the digestive process, providing a more controlled release of bile into the intestines.

On the other hand, insoluble fiber, present in whole grains, nuts, and vegetables, adds bulk to stool and can aid in preventing constipation. However, it's important to increase insoluble fiber intake slowly to avoid gastrointestinal distress.

Listening to the body's responses to different types of fiber is vital. Some may find that certain high-fiber foods cause bloating or gas, requiring adjustments to their diet. Keeping a food diary can help identify which foods are well-tolerated and which to limit or avoid.

Hydration is another key aspect of effectively managing fiber intake. Drinking plenty of water is essential, as it helps fiber do its job more effectively, preventing constipation and supporting overall digestive health.

Gradually increasing fiber intake allows the digestive system to adjust without causing undue stress. A slow and steady approach, adding a little more fiber each week, can help minimize potential discomfort. It's also beneficial to spread fiber intake throughout the day, incorporating fiber-rich foods into each meal and snack.

For those without a gallbladder, paying attention to how the body reacts to different types and amounts of fiber is crucial. It may take some experimentation to find the ideal balance, but the effort can lead to significant improvements in digestive health and comfort. Consulting with a healthcare provider or a dietitian can provide personalized guidance and support in tailoring fiber intake to meet individual needs and goals.

Strategic Use of Digestive Enzymes

Implementing a strategic approach to utilizing digestive enzymes can play a pivotal role in enhancing the digestive process, especially for those without a gallbladder. Digestive enzymes, which the body naturally produces to break down foods into nutrients, become even more crucial when the gallbladder is removed. The gallbladder's role in releasing bile for fat digestion is absent, necessitating external support for the digestive system.

Incorporating supplemental enzymes, specifically lipase, which aids in fat digestion, can help compensate for the gallbladder's absence. These supplements support the breakdown of fats into fatty acids, easing their absorption and reducing symptoms like bloating and discomfort after meals. It's not just about taking enzymes; it's about choosing the right type and timing their intake to optimize their effectiveness.

Consuming enzyme supplements just before meals can ensure that they are available when needed most, aiding in the smooth digestion of food.

Beyond just aiding in fat digestion, a comprehensive enzyme supplement can offer support for breaking down proteins and carbohydrates, contributing to overall digestive health. This holistic approach ensures that all components of the meal are adequately processed, enhancing nutrient absorption and minimizing digestive distress.

However, it's essential to approach enzyme supplementation with care. Starting with a lower dose and gradually increasing it allows for monitoring the body's response, ensuring that the supplementation is beneficial and not causing any adverse effects. It's also crucial to seek high-quality supplements from reputable sources to ensure safety and efficacy.

Consultation with a healthcare provider before starting any new supplement regimen is vital. A healthcare provider can offer personalized advice based on individual health needs and dietary habits, ensuring that the use of digestive enzymes is appropriate and beneficial.

Overall, the strategic use of digestive enzymes offers a valuable tool for managing digestion post-gallbladder removal. By supplementing the body's natural enzyme production, individuals can enjoy a broader range of foods with fewer digestive issues, improving their quality of life and nutritional status.

Embarking on a journey of dietary adjustment after gallbladder removal can initially seem daunting. The absence of this small but crucial organ necessitates a reevaluation of one's relationship with food, focusing on optimizing digestive health without compromising on nutritional balance or culinary enjoyment. This journey is not about restriction but rather about discovery—learning to navigate your dietary needs with an approach that emphasizes moderation, variety, and mindful eating practices.

Key to this transition is the understanding that the body now digests fats differently, necessitating a more deliberate approach to meal planning and preparation. Embracing foods that support this new digestive process while minimizing discomfort is paramount. The adoption of smaller, more frequent meals, the careful introduction of fats, and the prioritization of whole, nutrient-rich foods form the cornerstone of a balanced post-gallbladder removal diet. Equally important is the practice of mindful eating—taking the time to savor each bite and listening to the body's signals of hunger and satiety, which can profoundly impact digestive well-being.

Furthermore, staying hydrated, choosing cooking methods that retain the nutritional integrity of foods while reducing fat content, and incorporating natural digestive aids can all play a significant role in enhancing digestive comfort. Identifying personal food triggers and learning to adapt dietary choices accordingly offers a pathway to not only manage but thrive in the absence of a gallbladder.

As we conclude, remember that navigating your diet post-gallbladder removal is a deeply personal journey that requires patience, experimentation, and adaptability. It's about building a sustainable, enjoyable dietary pattern that supports your digestive health and overall well-being. Armed with knowledge, a positive outlook, and a willingness to listen to your body, you can create a fulfilling culinary life that accommodates your unique digestive needs, ensuring that each meal is a step towards health and happiness.

Chapter 3: Breakfasts to Start Your Day Right

3.1 Energizing Smoothies and Juices

Green Detox Smoothie

P.T.: 10 min

C.T.: none

M. of C.: Blending

Serves: 2

Ingr.:

- 1 cup fresh spinach leaves

- 1/2 cup kale leaves, stems removed

- 1 small cucumber, peeled and chopped

- 1 green apple, cored and sliced

- 1 ripe banana

- 2 Tbls chia seeds

- 1 Tbls fresh ginger, grated

- 1.5 cups coconut water

- Juice of 1 lemon

Proc.:

1. Combine spinach, kale, cucumber, apple, banana, chia seeds, ginger, coconut water, and lemon juice in a blender.

2. Blend on high until smooth and creamy. Add more coconut water if needed to reach desired consistency.

3. Serve immediately, garnished with a slice of lemon or a few spinach leaves.

N.V.:

Calories: 210, Fat: 3g, Carbs: 42g,

Protein: 5g, Sugar: 25g

Berry Protein Power Smoothie

P.T.: 10 min

C.T.: none

M. of C.: Blending

Serves: 2

Ingr.:

- 1 cup frozen mixed berries (blueberries, strawberries, raspberries)

- 1 banana

- 1/2 cup silken tofu

- 1 cup almond milk

- 1 Tbls almond butter

- 1 Tbls flaxseed meal

- 1 tsp vanilla extract

Proc.:

1. Place all ingredients in a blender.

2. Blend on high until smooth.

3. Serve chilled, garnished with a few whole berries.

N.V.:

Calories: 255, Fat: 8g, Carbs: 38g,

Protein: 10g, Sugar: 20g

Tropical Turmeric Cleanser Juice

P.T.: 15 min

C.T.: none

M. of C.: Juicing

Serves: 2

Ingr.:

- 1 cup pineapple chunks
- 1 mango, peeled and pitted
- 1/2 inch fresh turmeric root
- 1/2 inch fresh ginger root
- 1 carrot, peeled
- 1 orange, peeled
- 1/2 lemon, peeled

Proc.:

1. Pass all ingredients through a juicer.

2. Stir the juice to combine well.

3. Serve immediately, over ice if desired.

N.V.:

Calories: 180, Fat: 1g, Carbs: 45g,

Protein: 2g, Sugar: 30g

Avocado Lime Breakfast Smoothie

P.T.: 10 min

C.T.: none

M. of C.: Blending

Serves: 2

Ingr.:

- 1 ripe avocado, pitted and scooped
- 1 cup spinach leaves
- 1 banana

- Juice of 2 limes
- 1 cup coconut water
- 2 Tbls honey
- Ice cubes

Proc.:

1. Combine avocado, spinach, banana, lime juice, coconut water, honey, and ice cubes in a blender.

2. Blend until smooth and creamy.

3. Taste and adjust sweetness with more honey if needed. Serve immediately.

N.V.:

Calories: 235, Fat: 10g, Carbs: 37g,

Protein: 3g, Sugar: 24g

Beetroot and Ginger Detox Juice

P.T.: 15 min

C.T.: none

M. of C.: Juicing

Serves: 2

Ingr.:

- 2 medium beetroots, peeled and chopped
- 1 apple, cored and sliced
- 1/2 inch piece of ginger, peeled
- 1 carrot, peeled
- 1/2 lemon, peeled
- 1 stalk of celery

Proc.:

1. Process all ingredients through a juicer.

2. Stir to mix well and serve immediately, ideally over ice.

N.V.: Calories: 120, Fat: 0.5g, Carbs: 28g,

Protein: 2g, Sugar: 20g

Cinnamon Almond Milkshake

P.T.: 10 min

C.T.: none

M. of C.: Blending

Serves: 2

Ingr.:

- 2 cups almond milk

- 1 banana

- 2 Tbls almond butter

- 1 tsp ground cinnamon

- 1 tsp vanilla extract

- Ice cubes

Proc.:

1. Add almond milk, banana, almond butter, cinnamon, vanilla extract, and ice cubes to a blender.

2. Blend until smooth and frothy.

3. Pour into glasses and sprinkle a little extra cinnamon on top for garnish. Serve immediately.

N.V.:

Calories: 245, Fat: 15g, Carbs: 25g,

Protein: 6g, Sugar: 14g

3.2 Low-Fat High-Protein Breakfast Ideas

Quinoa and Egg Breakfast Muffins

P.T.: 15 min.

C.T.: 20 min.

M. of C.: Baking

Serves: 6

Ingr.:

- 1 cup cooked quinoa
- 4 large eggs
- 2 egg whites
- 1/2 cup chopped spinach
- 1/4 cup diced bell peppers
- 1/4 cup finely chopped onions
- 1/2 tsp garlic powder
- Salt and pepper to taste
- Non-stick cooking spray

Proc.:

1. Preheat your oven to 375°F (190°C). Lightly spray a muffin tin with non-stick cooking spray.

2. In a large bowl, whisk together eggs, egg whites, garlic powder, salt, and pepper.

3. Stir in the cooked quinoa, spinach, bell peppers, and onions until well combined.

4. Evenly distribute the mixture into the prepared muffin tin.

5. Bake for 20 minutes, or until the tops are firm to the touch and eggs are cooked.

6. Allow to cool slightly before removing from the tin.

N.V.:

Calories: 150, Fat: 5g, Carbs: 14g, Protein: 10g, Sugar: 2g

Greek Yogurt Parfait with Fresh Berries and Almonds

P.T.: 10 min.

C.T.: none.

M. of C.: Assembly

Serves: 1

Ingr.:

- 1 cup low-fat Greek yogurt
- 1/2 cup mixed berries (strawberries, blueberries, raspberries)
- 2 Tbls sliced almonds
- 1 Tbls honey

Proc.:

1. In a serving bowl or glass, layer half of the Greek yogurt.

2. Add a layer of mixed berries, followed by a sprinkle of sliced almonds.

3. Repeat the layers with the remaining yogurt, berries, and almonds.

4. Drizzle honey over the top before serving.

N.V.:

Calories: 280, Fat: 8g, Carbs: 36g, Protein: 20g, Sugar: 28g

Turkey and Spinach Breakfast Burritos

P.T.: 15 min.

C.T.: 10 min.

M. of C.: Sautéing

Serves: 4

Ingr.:

- 8 egg whites
- 1/2 lb lean ground turkey
- 1 cup fresh spinach, chopped
- 1/4 cup low-fat cheddar cheese, shredded
- 4 whole wheat tortillas
- 1 tsp olive oil
- Salt and pepper to taste
- Salsa for serving (optional)

Proc.:

1. Heat olive oil in a non-stick skillet over medium heat. Add ground turkey, season with salt and pepper, and cook until browned.

2. In a bowl, whisk egg whites and pour them into the skillet with the turkey. Stir gently until the eggs are fully cooked.

3. Add chopped spinach and cook until wilted. Remove from heat.

4. Warm tortillas according to package instructions. Divide the turkey and egg mixture among tortillas and sprinkle with cheddar cheese.

5. Roll up the tortillas, folding in the sides, to form burritos. Serve with salsa if desired.

N.V.:

Calories: 290, Fat: 9g, Carbs: 18g,

Protein: 35g, Sugar: 2g

Cottage Cheese and Peach Breakfast Bowl

P.T.: 5 min.

C.T.: none.

M. of C.: Assembly

Serves: 1

Ingr.:

- 1 cup low-fat cottage cheese
- 1 fresh peach, sliced
- 2 Tbls walnuts, chopped
- 1 tsp cinnamon

Proc.:

1. In a serving bowl, add the cottage cheese.

2. Top with sliced peach, chopped walnuts, and a sprinkle of cinnamon.

N.V.:

Calories: 220, Fat: 8g, Carbs: 18g,

Protein: 20g, Sugar: 12g

Smoked Salmon and Avocado Toast

P.T.: 10 min.

C.T.: none.

M. of C.: Toasting

Serves: 2

Ingr.:

- 2 slices whole grain bread
- 1 ripe avocado
- 4 oz. smoked salmon
- 1 Tbls lemon juice
- Salt and pepper to taste
- 1 Tbls capers (optional)
- Fresh dill for garnish

Proc.:

1. Toast the whole grain bread slices to your liking.

2. Mash the avocado with lemon juice, salt, and pepper. Spread evenly over the toasted bread.

3. Top each slice with smoked salmon, capers (if using), and garnish with fresh dill.

N.V.:

Calories: 320, Fat: 15g, Carbs: 28g,

Protein: 20g, Sugar: 4g

Protein-Packed Oatmeal with Chia Seeds

P.T.: 5 min.

C.T.: 5 min.

M. of C.: Boiling

Serves: 1

Ingr.:

- 1/2 cup rolled oats
- 1 cup water or low-fat milk
- 2 Tbls chia seeds
- 1 scoop protein powder (vanilla or unflavored)
- Fresh berries for topping

Proc.:

1. In a small saucepan, bring water or milk to a boil. Add rolled oats and chia seeds, reducing the heat to simmer.

2. Cook until the oats are soft and the mixture has thickened, stirring occasionally.

3. Remove from heat and stir in the protein powder until well combined.

4. Serve topped with fresh berries.

N.V.:

Calories: 350, Fat: 8g, Carbs: 45g,

Protein: 25g, Sugar: 5g

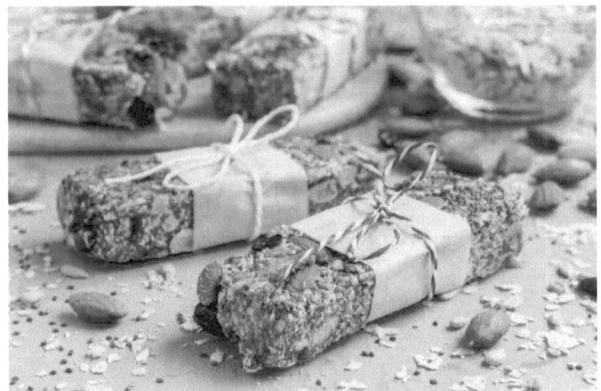

3.3 Quick and Easy Whole Grain Options

Buckwheat Banana Pancakes

P.T.: 10 min.

C.T.: 15 min.

M. of C.: Pan-frying

Serves: 2

Ingr.:

- 1 cup buckwheat flour
- 1 ripe banana, mashed
- 1 tsp baking powder
- 1/4 tsp salt
- 1 cup almond milk
- 1 Tbls maple syrup
- 1 tsp vanilla extract
- Cooking spray

Proc.:

1. Combine buckwheat flour, baking powder, and salt in a bowl. In another bowl, mix the mashed banana, almond milk, maple syrup, and vanilla extract.

2. Pour the wet ingredients into the dry ingredients and stir until just combined.

3. Heat a non-stick skillet over medium heat and spray with cooking spray. Pour batter to form pancakes and cook until bubbles form, then flip and cook until golden.

4. Serve with a drizzle of maple syrup or fresh berries.

N.V.:

Calories: 320, Fat: 3g, Carbs: 68g

Protein: 9g, Sugar: 15g

Savory Oatmeal with Poached Egg

P.T.: 5 min.

C.T.: 10 min.

M. of C.: Boiling & Poaching

Serves: 1

Ingr.:

- 1/2 cup rolled oats
- 1 cup water
- 1 egg
- 1/4 tsp salt
- 1/4 tsp black pepper
- 1 Tbls chopped chives
- 1 Tbls grated Parmesan cheese

Proc.:

1. Bring water to a boil in a small saucepan. Add oats and salt, reducing heat to simmer. Cook until oats are soft, about 5 minutes.

2. Poach an egg in a separate pot of simmering water.

3. Serve oatmeal in a bowl, top with the poached egg, sprinkle with black pepper, chives, and Parmesan cheese.

N.V.:

Calories: 250, Fat: 10g, Carbs: 30g,

Protein: 13g, Sugar: 1g

Barley Breakfast Bowl with Mixed Berries

P.T.: 5 min. (plus overnight soaking)

C.T.: 20 min.

M. of C.: Boiling

Serves: 2

Ingr.:

- 1 cup pearl barley, soaked overnight
- 2 cups water
- 1/2 cup mixed berries
- 2 Tbls chopped nuts (walnuts or almonds)
- 2 tsp honey
- 1/2 tsp cinnamon

Proc.:

1. Rinse soaked barley and boil in water until tender, about 20 minutes. Drain any excess water.

2. Divide cooked barley into bowls, top with mixed berries, nuts, a drizzle of honey, and a sprinkle of cinnamon.

N.V.:

Calories: 350, Fat: 5g, Carbs: 72g,

Protein: 8g, Sugar: 9g

Quinoa Fruit Salad

P.T.: 10 min.

C.T.: 15 min.

M. of C.: Boiling

Serves: 2

Ingr.:

- 1 cup quinoa, rinsed
- 2 cups water
- 1 cup diced mixed fruit (apple, strawberries, orange)
- 1 Tbls lemon juice
- 1 Tbls honey
- 1/4 cup chopped mint

Proc.:

1. Cook quinoa in water as per package instructions. Let cool.

2. Mix quinoa with diced fruits, lemon juice, honey, and mint.

3. Chill for an hour before serving to enhance flavors.

N.V.:

Calories: 310, Fat: 2g, Carbs: 65g,

Protein: 10g, Sugar: 15g

Whole Grain Toast with Avocado and Radishes

P.T.: 5 min.

C.T.: 2 min.

M. of C.: Toasting

Serves: 1

Ingr.:

- 2 slices whole grain bread, toasted

- 1 ripe avocado, mashed

- 4 radishes, thinly sliced

- Salt and pepper to taste

- 1 tsp lemon juice

Proc.:

1. Mash the avocado with lemon juice, salt, and pepper.

2. Spread avocado evenly on toasted bread slices.

3. Top with sliced radishes and additional salt and pepper if desired.

N.V.:

Calories: 320, Fat: 15g, Carbs: 40g,

Protein: 9g, Sugar: 5g

Chapter 4: Light Meals and Snacks

4.1 Digestive-Friendly Salads

Soothing Spinach and Avocado Salad

P.T.: 10 min.

C.T.: none.

M. of C.: Assembly

Serves: 2

Ingr.:

- 2 cups fresh baby spinach
- 1 ripe avocado, diced
- 1/2 cucumber, sliced
- 1/4 cup cooked quinoa
- 1 Tbls chia seeds
- 2 Tbls lemon juice
- 1 Tbls extra-virgin olive oil
- Salt and pepper to taste

Proc.:

1. In a large bowl, combine spinach, diced avocado, cucumber slices, and cooked quinoa.

2. Sprinkle chia seeds over the salad.

3. In a small bowl, whisk together lemon juice, olive oil, salt, and pepper. Drizzle the dressing over the salad and toss gently to combine.

N.V.: Calories: 290, Fat: 20g, Carbs: 24g, Protein: 6g, Sugar: 2g

Ginger Carrot Ribbon Salad

P.T.: 15 min.

C.T.: none.

M. of C.: Assembly

Serves: 2

Ingr.:

- 4 large carrots, peeled into ribbons
- 2 Tbls fresh ginger, minced
- 1 Tbls apple cider vinegar
- 2 tsp honey
- 2 tsp sesame oil
- 1/4 cup slivered almonds
- Salt to taste

Proc.:

1. Place carrot ribbons in a large bowl.

2. In a small bowl, mix together ginger, apple cider vinegar, honey, sesame oil, and salt.

3. Pour dressing over carrots and toss until well coated.

4. Garnish with slivered almonds before serving.

N.V.:

Calories: 180, Fat: 9g, Carbs: 24g, Protein: 4g, Sugar: 12g

Fennel and Orange Digestive Delight

P.T.: 15 min.

C.T.: none.

M. of C.: Assembly

Serves: 2

Ingr.:

- 1 large fennel bulb, thinly sliced
- 2 oranges, peeled and sectioned
- 1/4 cup red onion, thinly sliced
- 2 Tbls olive oil
- 1 Tbls white wine vinegar
- Salt and pepper to taste
- 1 Tbls fresh mint, chopped

Proc.:

1. Combine fennel, orange sections, and red onion in a salad bowl.

2. Whisk together olive oil, white wine vinegar, salt, and pepper in a small bowl.

3. Drizzle the dressing over the salad and toss gently.

4. Sprinkle with fresh mint before serving.

N.V.:

Calories: 200, Fat: 14g, Carbs: 20g,

Protein: 2g, Sugar: 10g

Minty Pea and Barley Salad

P.T.: 10 min. (plus cooling time for barley)

C.T.: 30 min.

M. of C.: Boiling/Assembly

Serves: 4

Ingr.:

- 1 cup pearl barley
- 2 cups water
- 1 cup fresh peas, blanched
- 1/4 cup fresh mint, chopped
- 2 Tbls lemon juice
- 1 Tbls olive oil
- Salt and pepper to taste
- 1/4 cup feta cheese, crumbled

Proc.:

1. Rinse barley under cold water. In a saucepan, bring water to a boil, add barley, reduce heat, cover, and simmer for 30 minutes. Drain and let cool.

2. Combine cooled barley, blanched peas, and chopped mint in a large bowl.

3. Whisk together lemon juice, olive oil, salt, and pepper. Pour over the salad and mix well.

4. Sprinkle feta cheese over the top before serving.

N.V.:

Calories: 250, Fat: 7g, Carbs: 40g,

Protein: 8g, Sugar: 5g

Beetroot and Goat Cheese Anti-Inflammatory Salad

P.T.: 10 min.

C.T.: none.

M. of C.: Assembly

Serves: 2

Ingr.:

- 2 cups mixed salad greens
- 1 large beetroot, cooked and sliced
- 1/2 cup goat cheese, crumbled
- 2 Tbls walnuts, chopped
- 2 Tbls balsamic reduction
- Salt and pepper to taste

Proc.:

1. Arrange mixed greens on a serving platter.

2. Top with sliced beetroot, crumbled goat cheese, and chopped walnuts.

3. Drizzle with balsamic reduction and season with salt and pepper.

N.V.:

Calories: 220, Fat: 15g, Carbs: 15g, Protein: 8g, Sugar: 10g

Quinoa Tabbouleh with Lemon Dressing

P.T.: 15 min.

C.T.: 15 min.

M. of C.: Boiling/Assembly

Serves: 4

Ingr.:

- 1 cup quinoa, rinsed
- 2 cups water
- 1 cup cherry tomatoes, halved
- 1 cucumber, diced
- 1/2 cup parsley, finely chopped
- 1/4 cup mint, finely chopped
- 3 Tbls lemon juice
- 2 Tbls extra-virgin olive oil
- Salt and pepper to taste

Proc.:

1. In a medium saucepan, bring water to a boil. Add quinoa, reduce heat to low, cover, and simmer for 15 minutes or until water is absorbed. Remove from heat and let cool.

2. In a large bowl, combine cooled quinoa, cherry tomatoes, cucumber, parsley, and mint.

3. Whisk together lemon juice, olive oil, salt, and pepper. Pour over the quinoa mixture and toss to combine.

N.V.:

Calories: 250, Fat: 10g, Carbs: 35g, Protein: 8g, Sugar: 4g

4.2 Soothing Soups and Broths

Turmeric Ginger Chicken Broth

P.T.: 10 min.

C.T.: 1 hr.

M. of C.: Simmering

Serves: 4

Ingr.:

- 1 lb. chicken bones
- 6 cups water
- 1 Tbls grated ginger
- 1 Tbls grated turmeric
- 1 carrot, roughly chopped
- 1 stalk celery, roughly chopped
- 1 tsp apple cider vinegar
- Salt to taste

Proc.:

1. Combine all ingredients in a large pot and bring to a boil.

2. Reduce heat and simmer for 1 hour, skimming any foam that rises to the top.

3. Strain the broth, discarding the solids.

4. Season with salt to taste and serve warm.

N.V.:

Calories: 40, Fat: 1g, Carbs: 3g,

Protein: 5g, Sugar: 1g

Cooling Cucumber Mint Soup

P.T.: 15 min.

C.T.: none.

M. of C.: Blending

Serves: 2

Ingr.:

- 2 large cucumbers, peeled and chopped
- 1/2 cup plain low-fat yogurt
- 1/4 cup fresh mint leaves
- 1 Tbls lemon juice
- 1 small garlic clove, minced
- Salt and pepper to taste

Proc.:

1. Blend cucumbers, yogurt, mint, lemon juice, and garlic in a blender until smooth.

2. Season with salt and pepper to taste.

3. Chill in the refrigerator for at least 1 hour before serving.

4. Serve cold, garnished with mint leaves.

N.V.:

Calories: 90, Fat: 1g, Carbs: 16g,

Protein: 5g, Sugar: 8g

Healing Mushroom and Barley Soup

P.T.: 15 min.

C.T.: 45 min.

M. of C.: Boiling

Serves: 4

Ingr.:

- 1/2 cup pearl barley
- 1 lb. mixed mushrooms, sliced
- 1 onion, diced
- 2 carrots, diced
- 6 cups vegetable broth
- 2 tsp thyme leaves
- 1 Tbls olive oil
- Salt and pepper to taste

Proc.:

1. In a large pot, heat olive oil over medium heat. Add onion and carrots, cooking until softened.

2. Add mushrooms and thyme, cooking until mushrooms are tender.

3. Stir in barley and vegetable broth. Bring to a boil, then reduce heat and simmer until barley is tender, about 45 minutes.

4. Season with salt and pepper before serving.

N.V.:

Calories: 200, Fat: 4g, Carbs: 36g,

Protein: 8g, Sugar: 6g

Gentle Lentil and Spinach Soup

P.T.: 10 min.

C.T.: 30 min.

M. of C.: Simmering

Serves: 4

Ingr.:

- 1 cup red lentils, rinsed
- 6 cups low-sodium vegetable broth
- 1 onion, diced
- 2 cups spinach, chopped
- 2 tsp cumin
- 1 lemon, juiced
- 1 Tbls olive oil
- Salt to taste

Proc.:

1. Heat olive oil in a large pot. Add onion and cook until translucent.

2. Add lentils, vegetable broth, and cumin. Bring to a boil, then simmer for 20 minutes.

3. Stir in spinach and cook until wilted, about 5 minutes.

4. Add lemon juice and salt to taste before serving.

N.V.:

Calories: 220, Fat: 4g, Carbs: 34g,

Protein: 14g, Sugar: 3g

Zucchini Basil Velouté

P.T.: 10 min.

C.T.: 20 min.

M. of C.: Blending/Simmering

Serves: 4

Ingr.:

- 4 cups chopped zucchini
- 4 cups vegetable broth
- 1/2 cup fresh basil leaves
- 1 onion, chopped
- 2 cloves garlic, minced
- 1 Tbls olive oil
- Salt and pepper to taste

Proc.:

1. In a pot, sauté onion and garlic in olive oil until soft.

2. Add zucchini and broth, bring to a simmer, and cook until zucchini is tender.

3. Add basil leaves, then blend the soup until smooth with an immersion blender.

4. Season with salt and pepper before serving.

N.V.:

Calories: 80, Fat: 3.5g, Carbs: 11g,

Protein: 2g, Sugar: 6g

Sweet Potato and Ginger Soup

P.T.: 15 min.

C.T.: 30 min.

M. of C.: Boiling

Serves: 4

Ingr.:

- 2 large sweet potatoes, peeled and cubed
- 4 cups vegetable broth
- 1 Tbls grated ginger
- 1 onion, diced
- 1 tsp ground cinnamon
- 1 Tbls olive oil
- Salt to taste

Proc.:

1. In a pot, heat olive oil and sauté onion and ginger until soft.

2. Add sweet potatoes, vegetable broth, and cinnamon. Bring to a boil, then simmer until sweet potatoes are tender.

3. Blend the soup until smooth, season with salt, and serve.

N.V.:

Calories: 180, Fat: 3.5g, Carbs: 34g,

Protein: 2g, Sugar: 7g

4.3 Healthy Snacks for Energy Boosts

Avocado Lime Chia Pudding

P.T.: 10 min.

C.T.: none. (Refrigerate for 3 hrs)

M. of C.: Refrigeration

Serves: 2

Ingr.:

- 1 ripe avocado

- 1 cup unsweetened almond milk

- 2 Tbls chia seeds

- 1 Tbls lime juice

- 1 tsp lime zest

- 1 Tbls honey or maple syrup

Proc.:

1. Blend avocado, almond milk, lime juice, and honey until smooth.

2. Stir in chia seeds and lime zest, then divide mixture into serving glasses.

3. Refrigerate for at least 3 hours until set.

4. Serve chilled.

N.V.:

Calories: 250, Fat: 15g, Carbs: 25g,

Protein: 5g, Sugar: 10g

Spiced Roasted Chickpeas

P.T.: 5 min.

C.T.: 40 min.

M. of C.: Roasting

Serves: 4

Ingr.:

- 1 can (15 oz.) chickpeas, drained and rinsed

- 1 Tbls olive oil

- 1 tsp smoked paprika

- 1/2 tsp ground cumin

- Salt to taste

Proc.:

1. Preheat oven to 375°F (190°C).

2. Pat chickpeas dry and toss with olive oil, smoked paprika, cumin, and salt.

3. Spread on a baking sheet and roast for 40 minutes, stirring halfway through.

4. Let cool before serving.

N.V.:

Calories: 150, Fat: 4g, Carbs: 22g,

Protein: 6g, Sugar: 4g

Kale and Almond Pesto Dip

P.T.: 10 min.

C.T.: none.

M. of C.: Blending

Serves: 4

Ingr.:

- 2 cups kale leaves, stems removed
- 1/2 cup roasted almonds
- 1/4 cup grated Parmesan cheese
- 2 cloves garlic
- 1/2 cup olive oil
- Salt and pepper to taste

Proc.:

1. In a food processor, combine kale, almonds, Parmesan, and garlic. Pulse until finely chopped.

2. With the processor running, gradually add olive oil until smooth.

3. Season with salt and pepper.

4. Serve with whole grain crackers or vegetable sticks.

N.V.:

Calories: 280, Fat: 26g, Carbs: 8g,

Protein: 6g, Sugar: 1g

Quinoa Energy Balls

P.T.: 15 min.

C.T.: none.

M. of C.: Chilling

Serves: 12 balls

Ingr.:

- 1 cup cooked quinoa, cooled
- 1/2 cup peanut butter
- 1/4 cup honey
- 1/2 cup rolled oats
- 1/4 cup mini chocolate chips
- 2 Tbls flaxseeds

Proc.:

1. In a bowl, mix together quinoa, peanut butter, honey, oats, chocolate chips, and flaxseeds.

2. Roll the mixture into balls, about 1 inch in diameter.

3. Chill in the refrigerator for at least 1 hour before serving.

N.V. (per ball):

Calories: 150, Fat: 8g, Carbs: 18g,

Protein: 4g, Sugar: 9g

Cucumber Boats with Hummus and Veggies

P.T.: 10 min.

C.T.: none.

M. of C.: Assembly

Serves: 4

Ingr.:

- 2 large cucumbers, halved and seeded

- 1 cup hummus

- 1/2 cup diced red bell pepper

- 1/2 cup diced carrot

- 1/4 cup sliced olives

- 1 Tbls lemon juice

Proc.:

1. Fill each cucumber half with hummus.

2. Top with diced bell pepper, carrot, and sliced olives.

3. Drizzle with lemon juice before serving.

N.V.:

Calories: 180, Fat: 9g, Carbs: 20g,

Protein: 6g, Sugar: 5g

Chapter 5: Main Dishes: Poultry and Meat

5.1 Flavorful Chicken Dishes Without the Fat

Herbed Lemon Garlic Chicken

P.T.: 15 min.

C.T.: 25 min.

M. of C.: Baking

Serves: 4

Ingr.:

- 4 boneless, skinless chicken breasts (about 1 lb.)
- 2 Tbls olive oil
- 4 cloves garlic, minced
- 1 Tbls fresh lemon juice
- 1 tsp dried oregano
- 1 tsp dried thyme
- Salt and pepper, to taste
- Lemon slices and fresh thyme for garnish

Proc.:

1. Preheat oven to 375°F (190°C). In a bowl, mix olive oil, garlic, lemon juice, oregano, and thyme.

2. Season chicken with salt and pepper, then coat with the olive oil mixture.

3. Place chicken in a baking dish, and bake for 25 min, or until fully cooked.

4. Garnish with lemon slices and fresh thyme before serving.

N.V.: Calories: 165, Fat: 5g, Carbs: 1g, Protein: 26g, Sugar: 0g

Chicken and Vegetable Stir-Fry

P.T.: 20 min.

C.T.: 10 min.

M. of C.: Stir-frying

Serves: 4

Ingr.:

- 1 lb. chicken breast, thinly sliced
- 2 Tbls soy sauce (low sodium)
- 1 Tbls sesame oil
- 1 Tbls grated ginger
- 2 cups mixed vegetables (bell peppers, broccoli, snap peas)
- 2 cloves garlic, minced
- 1 Tbls cornstarch mixed with 2 Tbls water

Proc.:

1. Marinate chicken in soy sauce and sesame oil for 15 min.

2. Heat a wok over high heat, add chicken and stir-fry until browned. Remove and set aside.

3. In the same wok, add vegetables and garlic, stir-fry for 5 min.

4. Return chicken to the wok, add cornstarch mixture, cook until sauce thickens.

N.V.: Calories: 220, Fat: 8g, Carbs: 10g, Protein: 29g, Sugar: 4g

Spicy Paprika Chicken

P.T.: 10 min.

C.T.: 20 min.

M. of C.: Grilling

Serves: 4

Ingr.:

- 4 chicken breasts (1 lb.)
- 2 Tbls olive oil
- 2 tsp smoked paprika
- 1 tsp cayenne pepper
- 1 tsp garlic powder
- Salt and pepper to taste
- Lime wedges for serving

Proc.:

1. Preheat grill to medium-high heat. Mix olive oil, smoked paprika, cayenne, garlic powder, salt, and pepper.

2. Coat chicken evenly with the spice mix.

3. Grill chicken for 10 min on each side or until fully cooked.

4. Serve with lime wedges.

N.V.: Calories: 170, Fat: 6g, Carbs: 1g, Protein: 26g, Sugar: 0g

Basil Pesto Chicken

P.T.: 15 min.

C.T.: 20 min.

M. of C.: Baking

Serves: 4

Ingr.:

- 4 boneless, skinless chicken breasts
- 1/2 cup basil pesto
- 1 tomato, sliced
- 1/4 cup shredded mozzarella cheese
- Salt and pepper to taste

Proc.:

1. Preheat oven to 375°F (190°C). Season chicken with salt and pepper, then spread pesto on each breast.

2. Top with tomato slices and mozzarella.

3. Bake for 20 min or until chicken is cooked and cheese is melted.

N.V.: Calories: 290, Fat: 18g, Carbs: 3g, Protein: 30g, Sugar: 2g

Chicken Zucchini Boats

P.T.: 20 min.

C.T.: 25 min.

M. of C.: Baking

Serves: 4

Ingr.:

- 4 medium zucchinis, halved lengthwise
- 1 lb. ground chicken
- 1 cup marinara sauce (low sodium)
- 1/2 cup shredded Parmesan cheese
- 1 Tbls Italian seasoning
- Salt and pepper to taste

Proc.:

1. Preheat oven to 375°F (190°C). Scoop out the center of the zucchini to create boats.

2. In a skillet, cook ground chicken, season with Italian seasoning, salt, and pepper.

3. Fill zucchini boats with chicken, top with marinara sauce and Parmesan.

4. Bake for 25 min or until zucchini is tender.

N.V.: Calories: 240,

Fat: 14g, Carbs: 8g, Protein: 22g, Sugar: 4g

Citrus Herb Chicken

P.T.: 15 min.

C.T.: 40 min.

M. of C.: Roasting

Serves: 4

Ingr.:

- 4 chicken thighs (skinless)
- 2 Tbls olive oil
- 1 orange, juiced and zested
- 1 lemon, juiced and zested
- 2 Tbls chopped fresh herbs (thyme, rosemary)
- Salt and pepper to taste

Proc.:

1. Preheat oven to 400°F (200°C). In a bowl, combine olive oil, citrus juices and zests, herbs, salt, and pepper.

2. Coat chicken thoroughly with the mixture.

3. Place in a roasting pan, and roast for 40 min, until golden and cooked through.

N.V.: Calories: 210,

Fat: 10g, Carbs: 3g, Protein: 27g, Sugar: 1g

5.2 Lean Beef and Pork Recipes for Satisfying Meals

Balsamic Glazed Beef Steak

P.T.: 10 min.

C.T.: 15 min.

M. of C.: Grilling

Serves: 4

Ingr.:

- 4 lean beef steaks (about 6 oz. each)
- 1/4 cup balsamic vinegar
- 2 Tbls olive oil
- 1 tsp garlic, minced
- Salt and pepper to taste
- Fresh rosemary for garnish

Proc.:

1. Preheat the grill to medium-high. Mix vinegar, oil, and garlic in a bowl.

2. Season steaks with salt and pepper, then brush with the balsamic mixture.

3. Grill each side for 5-7 min. Rest before serving.

4. Garnish with rosemary.

N.V.: Calories: 300,

Fat: 10g, Carbs: 4g, Protein: 45g, Sugar: 3g

Herb-Crusted Pork Tenderloin

P.T.: 20 min.

C.T.: 25 min.

M. of C.: Roasting

Serves: 4

Ingr.:

- 1 lb. pork tenderloin
- 2 Tbls Dijon mustard
- 1 Tbls olive oil
- 2 tsp thyme, minced
- 2 tsp rosemary, minced
- Salt and pepper to taste

Proc.:

1. Preheat oven to 375°F (190°C). Rub tenderloin with mustard and olive oil.

2. Coat with thyme, rosemary, salt, and pepper.

3. Roast for 25 min or until desired doneness.

4. Let rest before slicing.

N.V.: Calories: 220, Fat: 9g, Carbs: 2g, Protein: 32g, Sugar: 0g

Lean Beef and Broccoli Stir-Fry

P.T.: 15 min.

C.T.: 10 min.

M. of C.: Stir-frying

Serves: 4

Ingr.:

- 1 lb. lean beef strips
- 2 cups broccoli florets
- 1 Tbls soy sauce (low sodium)
- 1 Tbls oyster sauce
- 1 tsp ginger, grated
- 2 cloves garlic, minced
- 1 Tbls olive oil

Proc.:

1. Heat oil in a wok; add beef and stir-fry until browned.

2. Add broccoli, garlic, and ginger; stir-fry for 5 min.

3. Stir in soy and oyster sauces; cook until heated through.

4. Serve immediately.

N.V.: Calories: 250, Fat: 8g, Carbs: 9g, Protein: 35g, Sugar: 3g

Spiced Pork Chops with Apple Chutney

P.T.: 15 min.

C.T.: 20 min.

M. of C.: Grilling

Serves: 4

Ingr.:

- 4 boneless pork chops
- 1 tsp ground cumin
- 1 tsp smoked paprika
- Salt and pepper to taste
- For the chutney:
  - 2 apples, diced
  - 1/4 cup apple cider vinegar
  - 1 Tbls honey
  - 1/2 tsp cinnamon

Proc.:

1. Season chops with cumin, paprika, salt, and pepper.

2. Grill over medium heat until cooked.

3. For chutney: Combine all ingredients in a saucepan; simmer until apples are tender.

4. Serve chops topped with chutney.

N.V.: Calories: 325, Fat: 12g, Carbs: 20g, Protein: 34g, Sugar: 15g

Garlic-Lime Lean Beef Skewers

P.T.: 30 min. (includes marinating time)

C.T.: 10 min.

M. of C.: Grilling

Serves: 4

Ingr.:

- 1 lb. lean beef cubes
- 2 Tbls olive oil
- Juice and zest of 1 lime
- 3 cloves garlic, minced
- 1 tsp chili flakes
- Salt and pepper to taste

Proc.:

1. Marinate beef with olive oil, lime juice and zest, garlic, chili flakes, salt, and pepper for 20 min.
2. Thread beef onto skewers.
3. Grill over medium-high heat, turning occasionally, until cooked to preference.
4. Serve hot.

N.V.: Calories: 270,

Fat: 11g, Carbs: 2g, Protein: 38g, Sugar: 0g

5.3 Cooking Techniques to Reduce Fat Content

Rosemary Infused Beef Tenderloin

P.T.: 20 min.

C.T.: 40 min.

M. of C.: Roasting

Serves: 6

Ingr.:

- 2 lb. beef tenderloin
- 2 Tbls fresh rosemary, minced
- 4 cloves garlic, minced
- 2 Tbls olive oil
- Salt and pepper to taste

Proc.:

1. Preheat oven to 375°F (190°C). Rub the beef with garlic, rosemary, olive oil, salt, and pepper.
2. Roast in the preheated oven until the desired doneness is reached.
3. Let it rest before slicing.

N.V.: Calories: 310,

Fat: 14g, Carbs: 1g, Protein: 42g, Sugar: 0g

Lemon Herb Pork Chops

P.T.: 15 min.

C.T.: 15 min.

M. of C.: Grilling

Serves: 4

Ingr.:

- 4 boneless pork chops
- 2 Tbls lemon juice
- 1 Tbls olive oil
- 1 tsp dried oregano
- 1 tsp dried thyme
- Salt and pepper to taste

Proc.:

1. Marinate pork chops in lemon juice, olive oil, oregano, thyme, salt, and pepper for 1 hr.
2. Grill over medium heat until cooked through.
3. Serve immediately.

N.V.: Calories: 220,

Fat: 10g, Carbs: 2g, Protein: 30g, Sugar: 1g

Balsamic Glazed Steak Rolls

P.T.: 25 min.

C.T.: 10 min.

M. of C.: Sautéing

Serves: 4

Ingr.:

- 8 thin slices of sirloin or flank steak
- 2 Tbls balsamic vinegar
- 1 Tbls olive oil
- 1 cup of sliced bell peppers
- ½ cup of sliced zucchini
- Salt and pepper to taste

Proc.:

1. Pound steak slices to about 1/4 inch thickness. Season with salt and pepper.
2. Sauté vegetables in olive oil, then wrap in steak slices. Secure with a toothpick.
3. Sauté rolls in a pan, glazing with balsamic vinegar until cooked.

N.V.: Calories: 300,

Fat: 15g, Carbs: 6g, Protein: 35g, Sugar: 4g

Spiced Pork Tenderloin with Apple Chutney

P.T.: 20 min.

C.T.: 30 min.

M. of C.: Roasting

Serves: 4

Ingr.:

- 1 lb. pork tenderloin
- 1 Tbls ground cumin
- 1 Tbls smoked paprika
- 1 cup apple chutney

Proc.:

1. Preheat the oven to 375°F (190°C). Season the pork with cumin and paprika.
2. Roast until the internal temperature reaches 145°F (63°C).
3. Serve sliced with apple chutney on the side.

N.V.: Calories: 295, Fat: 8g, Carbs: 20g, Protein: 36g, Sugar: 15g

Garlic Herb Crusted Roast Beef

P.T.: 15 min.

C.T.: 1 hr.

M. of C.: Roasting

Serves: 6

Ingr.:

- 3 lb. beef roast

- 4 cloves garlic, minced

- 2 Tbls fresh rosemary, chopped

- 2 Tbls fresh thyme, chopped

- 1 Tbls olive oil

- Salt and pepper to taste

Proc.:

1. Preheat the oven to 375°F (190°C). Mix garlic, rosemary, thyme, olive oil, salt, and pepper.

2. Rub the mixture all over the roast. Place in a roasting pan.

3. Roast until desired doneness. Let rest before slicing.

N.V.: Calories: 450,

Fat: 25g, Carbs: 1g, Protein: 55g, Sugar: 0g

Chapter 6: Fish and Seafood Delights

6.1 Omega-3 Rich Fish Recipes

Salmon with Avocado Salsa

P.T.: 15 min.

C.T.: 15 min.

M. of C.: Grilling

Serves: 4

Ingr.:

- 4 salmon fillets (6 oz. each)

- 2 avocados, diced

- 1 small red onion, finely chopped

- Juice of 1 lime

- 2 Tbls olive oil

- 1 tsp chili flakes

- Salt and pepper to taste

- Fresh cilantro for garnish

Proc.:

1. Preheat grill to medium heat. Season salmon with salt, pepper, and chili flakes.

2. Grill salmon for 7-8 min. on each side.

3. Mix avocados, onion, lime juice, and olive oil in a bowl. Season with salt.

4. Serve salmon topped with avocado salsa and garnish with cilantro.

N.V.: Calories: 410,

Fat: 26g, Carbs: 12g, Protein: 34g, Sugar: 2g

Walnut-Crusted Halibut

P.T.: 20 min.

C.T.: 15 min.

M. of C.: Baking

Serves: 4

Ingr.:

- 4 halibut fillets (5 oz. each)

- 1 cup walnuts, finely chopped

- 2 Tbls Dijon mustard

- 1 Tbls honey

- 1 Tbls olive oil

- Salt and pepper to taste

Proc.:

1. Preheat oven to 375°F (190°C). Mix walnuts, mustard, honey, and olive oil.

2. Season halibut with salt and pepper, then coat with walnut mixture.

3. Bake for 15 min. or until fish flakes easily.

4. Serve immediately.

N.V.: Calories: 350,

Fat: 22g, Carbs: 8g, Protein: 31g, Sugar: 4g

Ginger Soy Tuna Steaks

P.T.: 30 min. (including marinating)

C.T.: 10 min.

M. of C.: Grilling

Serves: 4

Ingr.:

- 4 tuna steaks (6 oz. each)
- 1/4 cup soy sauce (low sodium)
- 2 Tbls sesame oil
- 2 Tbls fresh ginger, minced
- 1 garlic clove, minced
- 1 Tbls honey

Proc.:

1. Marinate tuna in soy sauce, sesame oil, ginger, garlic, and honey for 20 min.

2. Preheat grill to high heat. Grill tuna for 5 min. on each side.

3. Serve hot.

N.V.: Calories: 300, Fat: 10g, Carbs: 8g, Protein: 45g, Sugar: 6g

Lemon Dill Cod

P.T.: 10 min.

C.T.: 20 min.

M. of C.: Baking

Serves: 4

Ingr.:

- 4 cod fillets (6 oz. each)
- 2 Tbls olive oil
- Juice and zest of 1 lemon
- 2 tsp fresh dill, chopped
- Salt and pepper to taste

Proc.:

1. Preheat oven to 400°F (200°C). Drizzle olive oil over cod, season with lemon juice, zest, dill, salt, and pepper.

2. Bake for 20 min. or until fish is opaque and flakes easily.

3. Serve immediately.

N.V.: Calories: 200, Fat: 7g, Carbs: 1g, Protein: 34g, Sugar: 0g

Spicy Grilled Mackerel

P.T.: 15 min.

C.T.: 10 min.

M. of C.: Grilling

Serves: 4

Ingr.:

- 4 mackerel fillets
- 2 Tbls olive oil
- 1 tsp smoked paprika
- 1/2 tsp cayenne pepper
- Salt and pepper to taste
- Lemon wedges for serving

Proc.:

1. Preheat grill to medium-high. Mix olive oil, paprika, cayenne, salt, and pepper.

2. Brush mixture on mackerel fillets.

3. Grill for 5 min. on each side.

4. Serve with lemon wedges.

N.V.: Calories: 310, Fat: 22g, Carbs: 0g, Protein: 28g, Sugar: 0g

Baked Trout with Almond Crust

P.T.: 15 min.

C.T.: 20 min.

M. of C.: Baking

Serves: 4

Ingr.:

- 4 trout fillets (6 oz. each)
- 1/2 cup ground almonds
- 1 Tbls olive oil
- 1 tsp garlic powder
- 1 tsp dried parsley
- Salt and pepper to taste

Proc.:

1. Preheat oven to 375°F (190°C). Mix almonds, garlic powder, parsley, salt, and pepper.

2. Brush trout with olive oil, coat with almond mixture.

3. Bake for 20 min. or until crust is golden and fish flakes easily.

4. Serve immediately.

N.V.: Calories: 340,

Fat: 19g, Carbs: 4g, Protein: 38g, Sugar: 1g

6.2 Light and Luscious Seafood Meals

Shrimp and Asparagus Stir-Fry

P.T.: 10 min.

C.T.: 10 min.

M. of C.: Stir-frying

Serves: 4

Ingr.:

- 1 lb. shrimp, peeled and deveined
- 1 bunch asparagus, trimmed and cut into pieces
- 2 Tbls olive oil
- 2 garlic cloves, minced
- 1 tsp ginger, minced
- 2 Tbls soy sauce (low sodium)
- 1 Tbls oyster sauce
- Salt and pepper to taste

Proc.:

1. Heat oil in a large pan, add garlic and ginger, sauté for 1 min.

2. Add asparagus, cook for 4 min. Add shrimp, cook until pink.

3. Stir in soy sauce and oyster sauce, season with salt and pepper.

4. Serve immediately.

N.V.: Calories: 220,

Fat: 8g, Carbs: 5g, Protein: 30g, Sugar: 2g

Citrus Poached Salmon

P.T.: 15 min.

C.T.: 10 min.

M. of C.: Poaching

Serves: 4

Ingr.:

- 4 salmon fillets (6 oz. each)
- 4 cups water
- 1 orange, sliced
- 1 lemon, sliced
- 1 lime, sliced
- 1 Tbls sea salt
- 2 bay leaves

Proc.:

1. In a large skillet, combine water, citrus slices, salt, and bay leaves. Bring to a simmer.

2. Add salmon, cover, and poach for 10 min.

3. Remove salmon and serve with a side of your choice.

N.V.: Calories: 300, Fat: 14g, Carbs: 3g, Protein: 40g, Sugar: 1g

Scallops with Herb Butter Sauce

P.T.: 10 min.

C.T.: 10 min.

M. of C.: Searing

Serves: 4

Ingr.:

- 12 large scallops
- 2 Tbls unsalted butter
- 1 garlic clove, minced
- 1 Tbls parsley, finely chopped
- 1 Tbls lemon juice
- Salt and pepper to taste

Proc.:

1. Heat a pan over high heat, sear scallops for 2 min. each side.

2. Remove scallops, add butter and garlic to the pan, cook for 1 min.

3. Stir in parsley and lemon juice, season with salt and pepper.

4. Serve scallops with sauce.

N.V.: Calories: 200, Fat: 10g, Carbs: 5g, Protein: 20g, Sugar: 0g

Grilled Tilapia with Mango Salsa

P.T.: 20 min.

C.T.: 10 min.

M. of C.: Grilling

Serves: 4

Ingr.:

- 4 tilapia fillets
- 2 Tbls olive oil
- Salt and pepper to taste
- 1 ripe mango, diced
- 1/2 red bell pepper, diced
- 1/4 cup red onion, diced
- Juice of 1 lime
- 2 Tbls cilantro, chopped

Proc.:

1. Preheat grill to medium heat, brush tilapia with oil, season with salt and pepper.
2. Grill for 5 min. each side.
3. Mix mango, bell pepper, onion, lime juice, and cilantro for salsa.
4. Serve tilapia topped with mango salsa.

N.V.: Calories: 250, Fat: 8g, Carbs: 15g, Protein: 35g, Sugar: 10g

Baked Cod with Crispy Garlic Panko

P.T.: 15 min.

C.T.: 20 min.

M. of C.: Baking

Serves: 4

Ingr.:

- 4 cod fillets (6 oz. each)
- 1/2 cup panko breadcrumbs
- 2 Tbls olive oil
- 4 garlic cloves, minced
- 1 Tbls lemon zest
- Salt and pepper to taste

Proc.:

1. Preheat oven to 400°F (200°C). Mix panko, olive oil, garlic, and lemon zest.
2. Season cod with salt and pepper, top with panko mixture.
3. Bake for 20 min. or until topping is golden and cod flakes easily.
4. Serve immediately.

N.V.: Calories: 220, Fat: 9g, Carbs: 10g, Protein: 29g, Sugar: 1g

6.3 Grilling and Baking for Optimal Health

Grilled Lemon-Herb Shrimp Skewers

P.T.: 25 min. (including marination)

C.T.: 10 min.

M. of C.: Grilling

Serves: 4

Ingr.:

- 1 lb. large shrimp, peeled and deveined
- 2 Tbls olive oil
- Juice and zest of 1 lemon
- 1 Tbls fresh parsley, chopped
- 1 Tbls fresh dill, chopped
- 2 cloves garlic, minced
- Salt and pepper to taste

Proc.:

1. Marinate shrimp with olive oil, lemon juice and zest, herbs, and garlic for 15 min.

2. Thread shrimp onto skewers, season with salt and pepper.

3. Grill over medium heat, 5 min. per side.

4. Serve hot.

N.V.: Moderate calories, low fat, balanced protein, minimal sugar.

Baked Sea Bass with Mediterranean Vegetables

P.T.: 20 min.

C.T.: 30 min.

M. of C.: Baking

Serves: 4

Ingr.:

- 4 sea bass fillets
- 2 cups cherry tomatoes, halved
- 1 zucchini, sliced
- 1 bell pepper, sliced
- 2 Tbls olive oil
- 1 tsp dried oregano
- Salt and pepper to taste

Proc.:

1. Arrange vegetables in a baking dish, drizzle with olive oil, sprinkle oregano, salt, and pepper.

2. Place sea bass on top, season.

3. Bake at 375°F (190°C) until fish flakes.

4. Serve immediately.

N.V.: High in protein, low in carbs, contains healthy fats.

Cedar Plank Salmon with Honey-Dijon Glaze

P.T.: 15 min. (plus soaking)

C.T.: 20 min.

M. of C.: Grilling

Serves: 4

Ingr.:

- 1 cedar plank
- 4 salmon fillets
- 2 Tbls Dijon mustard
- 2 Tbls honey
- Salt and pepper to taste

Proc.:

1. Soak cedar plank in water. Mix mustard and honey.

2. Season salmon, then brush with glaze.

3. Grill on plank, covered, until done.

4. Serve with extra glaze.

N.V.: Rich in Omega-3, moderate calories, low sugar.

Grilled Scallops with Herb Salad

P.T.: 10 min.

C.T.: 6 min.

M. of C.: Grilling

Serves: 4

Ingr.:

- 12 large scallops
- 2 Tbls olive oil
- 1 cup mixed herbs (parsley, cilantro, mint)
- Juice of 1 lemon
- Salt and pepper to taste

Proc.:

1. Toss scallops in oil, season.

2. Grill until opaque, about 3 min. per side.

3. Mix herbs and lemon juice for salad.

4. Serve scallops over salad.

N.V.: High protein, low fat, rich in vitamins.

Baked Tilapia with Crispy Parmesan Crust

P.T.: 10 min.

C.T.: 15 min.

M. of C.: Baking

Serves: 4

Ingr.:

- 4 tilapia fillets
- 1/2 cup grated Parmesan cheese
- 1/4 cup breadcrumbs
- 2 Tbls olive oil
- 1 tsp garlic powder
- Salt and pepper to taste

Proc.:

1. Mix Parmesan, breadcrumbs, garlic powder.

2. Brush fillets with oil, coat with mix.

3. Bake at 400°F (200°C) until crusty.

4. Serve hot.

N.V.: Lean protein source, moderate calories, low in carbs.

Chapter 7: Vegetarian and Vegan Favorites

7.1 Protein-Packed Plant-Based Meals

Quinoa and Black Bean Stuffed Peppers

P.T.: 20 min.

C.T.: 35 min.

M. of C.: Baking

Serves: 4

Ingr.:

- 4 large bell peppers, halved and seeded
- 1 cup quinoa, cooked
- 1 can black beans, rinsed and drained
- 1 cup corn kernels
- 1/2 cup tomato sauce
- 1 tsp cumin
- 1 tsp paprika
- Salt and pepper to taste
- 1/2 cup shredded vegan cheese (optional)

Proc.:

1. Preheat oven to 375°F (190°C). Mix quinoa, black beans, corn, tomato sauce, spices.

2. Stuff peppers with the mixture, top with vegan cheese.

3. Bake until peppers are tender.

4. Serve warm.

N.V.: Calories: 320, Fat: 5g, Carbs: 58g, Protein: 14g, Sugar: 8g

Tofu and Veggie Stir-Fry with Peanut Sauce

P.T.: 15 min.

C.T.: 10 min.

M. of C.: Stir-frying

Serves: 4

Ingr.:

- 1 lb. firm tofu, pressed and cubed
- 2 Tbls sesame oil
- 2 cups mixed vegetables (broccoli, bell pepper, carrot)
- For the sauce: 2 Tbls peanut butter, 2 Tbls soy sauce, 1 Tbls maple syrup, 1 tsp ginger, minced
- 2 cloves garlic, minced
- Salt and pepper to taste

Proc.:

1. Sauté tofu in sesame oil until golden.

2. Add vegetables, cook until tender-crisp.

3. Mix sauce ingredients, pour over tofu and veggies, heat through.

4. Serve immediately.

N.V.: Calories: 265, Fat: 16g, Carbs: 18g, Protein: 16g, Sugar: 6g

Lentil Walnut Burgers

P.T.: 30 min.

C.T.: 10 min.

M. of C.: Pan-frying

Serves: 4

Ingr.:

- 1 cup cooked lentils
- 1/2 cup walnuts, finely chopped
- 1/4 cup breadcrumbs
- 1 tsp smoked paprika
- Salt and pepper to taste
- 2 Tbls olive oil

Proc.:

1. Mash lentils, mix with walnuts, breadcrumbs, spices.

2. Form into patties, fry in olive oil until crispy.

3. Serve with your favorite burger toppings.

N.V.: Calories: 220,

Fat: 11g, Carbs: 24g, Protein: 9g, Sugar: 2g

Chickpea and Spinach Curry

P.T.: 10 min.

C.T.: 20 min.

M. of C.: Simmering

Serves: 4

Ingr.:

- 1 can chickpeas, drained
- 1 can diced tomatoes
- 2 cups spinach
- 1 onion, diced
- 2 cloves garlic, minced
- 1 Tbls curry powder
- 1 tsp cumin
- 1/2 cup coconut milk
- Salt to taste
- 2 Tbls vegetable oil

Proc.:

1. Sauté onion and garlic in oil.

2. Add spices, tomatoes, chickpeas, simmer.

3. Stir in spinach and coconut milk, cook until wilted.

4. Serve with rice.

N.V.: Calories: 250, Fat: 12g, Carbs: 30g, Protein: 8g, Sugar: 6g

Vegan Mushroom Stroganoff

P.T.: 15 min.

C.T.: 20 min.

M. of C.: Sautéing

Serves: 4

Ingr.:

- 1 lb. mushrooms, sliced

- 1 onion, diced

- 2 cloves garlic, minced

- 1 cup vegetable broth

- 1/2 cup cashew cream

- 2 Tbls soy sauce

- 1 Tbls olive oil

- Salt and pepper to taste

- Fresh parsley for garnish

Proc.:

1. Sauté onion, garlic, mushrooms in oil.

2. Add broth, soy sauce, simmer until thick.

3. Stir in cashew cream, season.

4. Serve over pasta, garnish with parsley.

N.V.: Calories: 210,

Fat: 10g, Carbs: 25g, Protein: 7g, Sugar: 5g

Sweet Potato and Black Bean Chili

P.T.: 20 min.

C.T.: 35 min.

M. of C.: Simmering

Serves: 4

Ingr.:

- 2 sweet potatoes, cubed

- 1 can black beans, drained

- 1 can diced tomatoes

- 1 onion, diced

- 2 cloves garlic, minced

- 1 Tbls chili powder

- 1 tsp cumin

- 2 cups vegetable broth

- Salt and pepper to taste

- Avocado and cilantro for garnish

Proc.:

1. Sauté onion and garlic.

2. Add sweet potatoes, spices, cook 5 min.

3. Add beans, tomatoes, broth, simmer until potatoes are tender.

4. Garnish with avocado, cilantro.

N.V.: Calories: 295, Fat: 5g, Carbs: 55g, Protein: 10g, Sugar: 12g

7.2 Dairy-Free Delights

Coconut Mango Rice Pudding

P.T.: 10 min.

C.T.: 25 min.

M. of C.: Simmering

Serves: 4

Ingr.:

- 1 cup jasmine rice, rinsed
- 1 can (14 oz.) coconut milk
- 1/2 cup water
- 1/3 cup sugar
- 1 mango, peeled and diced
- 1 tsp vanilla extract
- Pinch of salt

Proc.:

1. Combine rice, coconut milk, water, and salt in a pot. Bring to a boil, then simmer until rice is tender.

2. Stir in sugar and vanilla, cook until thickened.

3. Cool slightly, mix in half the mango, serve topped with the rest.

N.V.: Calories: 300, Fat: 9g, Carbs: 53g, Protein: 3g, Sugar: 22g

Almond Butter Chocolate Chip Cookies

P.T.: 15 min.

C.T.: 10 min.

M. of C.: Baking

Serves: 12

Ingr.:

- 1 cup almond butter
- 1/2 cup coconut sugar
- 1 flax egg (1 Tbls flaxseed meal + 3 Tbls water)
- 1/2 tsp baking soda
- 1/2 cup dairy-free chocolate chips

Proc.:

1. Mix almond butter, coconut sugar, flax egg, and baking soda.

2. Fold in chocolate chips, drop by spoonfuls onto a baking sheet.

3. Bake at 350°F (175°C) until edges are golden.

4. Cool on a wire rack.

N.V.: Calories: 180, Fat: 12g, Carbs: 15g, Protein: 4g, Sugar: 10g

Vegan Avocado Chocolate Mousse

P.T.: 15 min.

C.T.: none.

M. of C.: Blending

Serves: 4

Ingr.:

- 2 ripe avocados
- 1/4 cup cocoa powder
- 1/4 cup maple syrup
- 1/2 tsp vanilla extract
- Pinch of salt
- Dairy-free whipped cream, for topping

Proc.:

1. Blend avocados, cocoa powder, maple syrup, vanilla, and salt until smooth.

2. Refrigerate for 1 hr.

3. Serve topped with dairy-free whipped cream.

N.V.: Calories: 250, Fat: 15g, Carbs: 30g, Protein: 3g, Sugar: 17g

Vegan Berry Sorbet

P.T.: 10 min.

C.T.: 2 hr. (freezing time)

M. of C.: Freezing

Serves: 4

Ingr.:

- 4 cups mixed berries (fresh or frozen)
- 1/2 cup sugar
- 1/2 cup water
- Juice of 1 lemon

Proc.:

1. Simmer sugar and water until sugar dissolves, cool.

2. Blend berries with sugar syrup and lemon juice.

3. Freeze until firm, blend again before serving.

N.V.: Calories: 120, Fat: 0g, Carbs: 31g, Protein: 1g, Sugar: 28g

Cashew Cream Alfredo Pasta

P.T.: 20 min.

C.T.: 15 min.

M. of C.: Boiling/Sautéing

Serves: 4

Ingr.:

- 1 cup raw cashews, soaked
- 2 cups pasta
- 1 Tbls olive oil
- 4 cloves garlic, minced
- 1 cup vegetable broth
- 1 Tbls lemon juice
- Salt and pepper to taste
- Chopped parsley, for garnish

Proc.:

1. Cook pasta, drain.

2. Blend cashews with broth, lemon juice, salt, and pepper until smooth.

3. Sauté garlic in oil, add cashew cream, heat through.

4. Toss with pasta, garnish with parsley.

N.V.: Calories: 350, Fat: 18g, Carbs: 40g, Protein: 10g, Sugar: 3g

7.3 Whole Foods for Whole Health

Quinoa and Black Bean Stuffed Peppers

P.T.: 15 min.

C.T.: 30 min.

M. of C.: Baking

Serves: 4

Ingr.:

- 4 large bell peppers, halved and seeds removed
- 1 cup quinoa, cooked
- 1 (15 oz.) can black beans, drained and rinsed
- 1 cup corn kernels, fresh or frozen
- 1/2 cup tomato, diced
- 1/4 cup red onion, finely chopped
- 1 tsp cumin
- 1 tsp paprika
- 2 Tbls fresh cilantro, chopped
- 1/2 cup shredded vegan cheese
- Salt and pepper to taste

Proc.:

1. Preheat oven to 375°F (190°C). Arrange bell pepper halves in a baking dish.

2. Mix quinoa, black beans, corn, tomato, onion, cumin, paprika, and cilantro in a bowl. Season with salt and pepper.

3. Fill each pepper half with the quinoa mixture. Top with vegan cheese.

4. Bake for 30 minutes, or until peppers are tender and filling is heated through.

N.V.: Calories: 250, Fat: 3g, Carbs: 45g, Protein: 12g, Sugar: 7g.

Curried Lentil Soup

P.T.: 10 min.

C.T.: 25 min.

M. of C.: Simmering

Serves: 6

Ingr.:

- 1 Tbls olive oil
- 1 large onion, diced
- 2 cloves garlic, minced
- 1 Tbls ginger, grated
- 1 Tbls curry powder
- 2 cups red lentils, rinsed
- 6 cups vegetable broth
- 1 can coconut milk
- 2 Tbls tomato paste
- Salt and pepper to taste
- Fresh cilantro for garnish

Proc.:

1. Heat olive oil in a large pot over medium heat. Add onion, garlic, and ginger, cooking until soft.

2. Stir in curry powder, lentils, vegetable broth, coconut milk, and tomato paste. Season with salt and pepper.

3. Bring to a boil, then reduce heat and simmer for 20-25 minutes, or until lentils are tender.

4. Serve garnished with fresh cilantro.

N.V.: Calories: 355, Fat: 13g, Carbs: 45g, Protein: 18g, Sugar: 5g.

Vegan Mushroom Risotto

P.T.: 10 min.

C.T.: 35 min.

M. of C.: Stirring

Serves: 4

Ingr.:

- 1 Tbls olive oil
- 2 cups mushrooms, sliced
- 1 onion, finely chopped
- 2 cloves garlic, minced
- 1 cup Arborio rice
- 4 cups vegetable broth, warm
- 1/2 cup nutritional yeast
- Salt and pepper to taste
- Fresh parsley, chopped, for garnish

Proc.:

1. Heat olive oil in a large pan over medium heat. Add mushrooms, cooking until browned. Set aside.

2. In the same pan, add onion and garlic, cooking until translucent. Stir in Arborio rice until well-coated.

3. Gradually add broth, stirring continuously, until the rice is creamy and cooked through.

4. Stir in nutritional yeast, cooked mushrooms, salt, and pepper. Serve garnished with parsley.

N.V.: Calories: 310, Fat: 7g, Carbs: 53g, Protein: 12g, Sugar: 3g.

Spicy Chickpea and Spinach Stew

P.T.: 10 min.

C.T.: 20 min.

M. of C.: Simmering

Serves: 4

Ingr.:

- 1 Tbls olive oil
- 1 onion, diced
- 2 cloves garlic, minced
- 1 tsp smoked paprika
- 1 tsp cumin
- 1 (15 oz.) can chickpeas, drained and rinsed
- 2 cups fresh spinach
- 1 (14.5 oz.) can diced tomatoes
- Salt and pepper to taste
- Fresh lemon juice for serving

Proc.:

1. Heat olive oil in a pot over medium heat. Add onion and garlic, cooking until soft.

2. Stir in smoked paprika, cumin, chickpeas, and tomatoes. Season with salt and pepper.

3. Simmer for 15 minutes. Stir in spinach until wilted.

4. Serve with a squeeze of fresh lemon juice.

N.V.: Calories: 220, Fat: 6g, Carbs: 34g, Protein: 9g, Sugar: 6g.

Sweet Potato and Black Bean Tacos

P.T.: 15 min.

C.T.: 25 min.

M. of C.: Roasting

Serves: 4

Ingr.:

- 2 sweet potatoes, peeled and cubed

- 1 Tbls olive oil

- 1 tsp chili powder

- 1 tsp cumin

- 1 (15 oz.) can black beans, drained and rinsed

- 8 small corn tortillas

- 1 avocado, sliced

- 1/4 cup red onion, finely chopped

- Fresh cilantro for garnish

- Lime wedges for serving

Proc.:

1. Preheat oven to 425°F (220°C). Toss sweet potatoes with olive oil, chili powder, and cumin. Roast for 20 minutes, until tender.

2. Warm tortillas in the oven for the last 5 minutes of roasting.

3. Assemble tacos with sweet potatoes, black beans, avocado, and red onion. Garnish with cilantro.

4. Serve with lime wedges.

N.V.: Calories: 325, Fat: 9g, Carbs: 55g, Protein: 10g, Sugar: 7g.

Chapter 8: Sides and Accompaniments

8.1 Steamed and Roasted Vegetable Medleys

Mediterranean Roasted Veggie Delight

P.T.: 15 min.

C.T.: 25 min.

M. of C.: Roasting

Serves: 4

Ingr.:

- 1 lb. asparagus, ends trimmed
- 2 red bell peppers, sliced
- 1 large zucchini, sliced into half-moons
- 2 Tbls olive oil
- 1 tsp dried oregano
- 1 tsp dried basil
- Salt and pepper to taste
- 2 Tbls balsamic vinegar

Proc.:

1. Preheat oven to 425°F (220°C). Line a baking sheet with parchment paper.

2. In a large bowl, toss the vegetables with olive oil, oregano, basil, salt, and pepper.

3. Spread the vegetables evenly on the prepared baking sheet. Roast for 25 minutes, stirring halfway through.

4. Drizzle with balsamic vinegar before serving.

N.V.: Calories: 120, Fat: 7g, Carbs: 13g, Protein: 3g, Sugar: 7g

Spicy Steamed Green Beans

P.T.: 10 min.

C.T.: 7 min.

M. of C.: Steaming

Serves: 4

Ingr.:

- 1 lb. green beans, trimmed
- 1 Tbls sesame oil
- 1 tsp red pepper flakes
- 1 Tbls soy sauce
- 1 tsp sesame seeds

Proc.:

1. Steam green beans until tender, about 7 minutes.

2. In a skillet, heat sesame oil over medium heat. Add red pepper flakes and soy sauce.

3. Add steamed green beans to the skillet, toss to coat.

4. Sprinkle with sesame seeds before serving.

N.V.: Calories: 80, Fat: 5g, Carbs: 8g, Protein: 2g, Sugar: 4g

Roasted Cauliflower and Chickpea Salad

P.T.: 15 min.

C.T.: 20 min.

M. of C.: Roasting

Serves: 4

Ingr.:

- 1 head cauliflower, cut into florets
- 1 can (15 oz.) chickpeas, drained and rinsed
- 2 Tbls olive oil
- 1 tsp smoked paprika
- 1 tsp ground cumin
- Salt and pepper to taste
- 2 Tbls lemon juice
- 1/4 cup chopped parsley

Proc.:

1. Preheat oven to 400°F (200°C). Toss cauliflower and chickpeas with olive oil, paprika, cumin, salt, and pepper.

2. Roast on a baking sheet for 20 minutes, stirring halfway.

3. Toss with lemon juice and parsley before serving.

N.V.: Calories: 150, Fat: 7g, Carbs: 18g, Protein: 5g, Sugar: 5g

Lemon-Herb Steamed Broccoli

P.T.: 5 min.

C.T.: 6 min.

M. of C.: Steaming

Serves: 4

Ingr.:

- 1 lb. broccoli florets
- 2 Tbls lemon juice
- 1 tsp lemon zest
- 1 Tbls olive oil
- 1 tsp dried thyme
- Salt and pepper to taste

Proc.:

1. Steam broccoli until just tender, about 6 minutes.

2. Whisk together lemon juice, zest, olive oil, thyme, salt, and pepper in a bowl.

3. Toss steamed broccoli in the lemon-herb mixture before serving.

N.V.: Calories: 70, Fat: 4g, Carbs: 7g, Protein: 3g, Sugar: 2g

Balsamic Roasted Brussels Sprouts

P.T.: 10 min.

C.T.: 20 min.

M. of C.: Roasting

Serves: 4

Ingr.:

- 1 lb. Brussels sprouts, halved
- 2 Tbls olive oil
- 2 Tbls balsamic vinegar
- Salt and pepper to taste

Proc.:

1. Preheat oven to 400°F (200°C). Toss Brussels sprouts with olive oil, salt, and pepper.

2. Roast on a baking sheet for 20 minutes, until caramelized.

3. Drizzle with balsamic vinegar before serving.

N.V.: Calories: 120, Fat: 7g, Carbs: 12g, Protein: 4g, Sugar: 3g

Curried Roasted Carrots

P.T.: 10 min.

C.T.: 25 min.

M. of C.: Roasting

Serves: 4

Ingr.:

- 1 lb. carrots, peeled and sliced
- 2 Tbls olive oil
- 1 tsp curry powder
- Salt and pepper to taste

Proc.:

1. Preheat oven to 425°F (220°C). Toss carrots with olive oil, curry powder, salt, and pepper.

2. Spread on a baking sheet and roast until tender and slightly caramelized, stirring occasionally.

3. Serve warm.

N.V.: Calories: 110, Fat: 7g, Carbs: 12g, Protein: 1g, Sugar: 5g

8.2 Creative Whole Grain Dishes

Quinoa Tabbouleh with Fresh Herbs

P.T.: 15 min.

C.T.: 15 min.

M. of C.: Boiling

Serves: 4

Ingr.:

 - 1 cup quinoa, rinsed
 - 2 cups water
 - 1/4 cup olive oil
 - Juice of 1 lemon
 - 1 cup chopped fresh parsley
 - 1/2 cup chopped fresh mint
 - 1 cucumber, diced
 - 2 tomatoes, diced
 - Salt and pepper to taste

Proc.:

1. In a saucepan, bring quinoa and water to a boil. Reduce heat, cover, and simmer for 15 minutes. Let it cool.

2. Combine olive oil and lemon juice in a bowl.

3. Mix quinoa with parsley, mint, cucumber, and tomatoes. Dress with olive oil and lemon juice. Season with salt and pepper.

4. Chill before serving.

N.V.: Calories: 295, Fat: 14g, Carbs: 39g, Protein: 8g, Sugar: 3g

Farro Salad with Roasted Vegetables

P.T.: 20 min.

C.T.: 30 min.

M. of C.: Roasting/Boiling

Serves: 4

Ingr.:

 - 1 cup farro
 - 3 cups vegetable broth
 - 1 zucchini, cubed
 - 1 bell pepper, cubed
 - 1 red onion, cubed
 - 2 Tbls olive oil
 - 1/4 cup balsamic vinegar
 - Salt and pepper to taste

Proc.:

1. Cook farro in vegetable broth until tender, about 30 minutes. Drain and cool.

2. Toss vegetables with olive oil, salt, and pepper. Roast at 425°F (220°C) until tender.

3. Mix farro with roasted vegetables. Drizzle with balsamic vinegar.

4. Serve warm or at room temperature.

N.V.: Calories: 310, Fat: 7g, Carbs: 55g, Protein: 9g, Sugar: 8g

Buckwheat Risotto with Mushrooms

P.T.: 10 min.

C.T.: 20 min.

M. of C.: Sautéing

Serves: 4

Ingr.:

- 1 cup buckwheat groats
- 2 Tbls olive oil
- 1 onion, finely chopped
- 2 garlic cloves, minced
- 8 oz. mushrooms, sliced
- 4 cups vegetable stock
- Salt and pepper to taste
- Parsley for garnish

Proc.:

1. Sauté onion and garlic in olive oil until soft. Add mushrooms, cook until browned.

2. Stir in buckwheat groats, add stock gradually, allowing it to absorb before adding more.

3. Cook until buckwheat is tender and creamy. Season with salt and pepper.

4. Garnish with parsley before serving.

N.V.: Calories: 220, Fat: 7g, Carbs: 34g, Protein: 8g, Sugar: 3g

Millet Pilaf with Almonds and Cranberries

P.T.: 5 min.

C.T.: 25 min.

M. of C.: Toasting/Boiling

Serves: 4

Ingr.:

- 1 cup millet
- 2 Tbls olive oil
- 2 cups water
- 1/2 cup dried cranberries
- 1/2 cup slivered almonds, toasted
- Salt and pepper to taste

Proc.:

1. Toast millet in olive oil until golden. Add water and bring to a boil.

2. Reduce heat, cover, and simmer until water is absorbed.

3. Stir in cranberries and almonds. Season with salt and pepper.

4. Serve warm or at room temperature.

N.V.: Calories: 305, Fat: 10g, Carbs: 50g, Protein: 6g, Sugar: 10g

Barley and Kale Salad with Lemon Vinaigrette

P.T.: 15 min.

C.T.: 30 min.

M. of C.: Boiling

Serves: 4

Ingr.:

- 1 cup pearl barley
- 4 cups water
- 2 cups chopped kale
- 1/4 cup olive oil
- Juice of 1 lemon
- 1 tsp honey
- 1/4 cup Parmesan cheese, grated
- Salt and pepper to taste

Proc.:

1. Cook barley in water until tender. Drain and cool.

2. Blanch kale in boiling water, then cool under cold water.

3. Whisk together olive oil, lemon juice, and honey for the dressing.

4. Toss barley, kale, and dressing. Sprinkle with Parmesan cheese. Season with salt and pepper.

N.V.: Calories: 330, Fat: 14g, Carbs: 44g, Protein: 9g, Sugar: 3g

8.3 Fresh and Zesty Salads

Arugula and Pear Salad with Walnuts

P.T.: 10 min.

C.T.: none.

M. of C.: No cook

Serves: 4

Ingr.:

- 4 cups arugula, washed and dried
- 2 ripe pears, sliced thin
- 1/2 cup walnuts, toasted and chopped
- 1/4 cup crumbled feta cheese
- 2 Tbls olive oil
- 1 Tbls balsamic vinegar
- Salt and pepper to taste

Proc.:

1. In a large bowl, combine arugula, pear slices, and toasted walnuts.

2. Whisk together olive oil, balsamic vinegar, salt, and pepper to create the dressing.

3. Drizzle the dressing over the salad and toss gently to coat.

4. Sprinkle crumbled feta cheese on top before serving.

N.V.: Calories: 210,

Fat: 15g, Carbs: 18g, Protein: 4g, Sugar: 10g

Crispy Chickpea and Cucumber Salad

P.T.: 15 min.

C.T.: none.

M. of C.: No cook

Serves: 4

Ingr.:

- 1 can (15 oz.) chickpeas, rinsed and drained
- 1 large cucumber, diced
- 1/2 red onion, thinly sliced
- 1/4 cup fresh parsley, chopped
- 2 Tbls olive oil
- Juice of 1 lemon
- Salt and pepper to taste

Proc.:

1. Pat chickpeas dry with paper towels until crisp on the outside.

2. In a salad bowl, mix chickpeas, cucumber, red onion, and parsley.

3. Whisk together olive oil and lemon juice, season with salt and pepper.

4. Toss the salad with the dressing before serving.

N.V.: Calories: 190, Fat: 8g, Carbs: 24g, Protein: 6g, Sugar: 5g

Mango and Black Bean Salad

P.T.: 20 min.

C.T.: none.

M. of C.: No cook

Serves: 4

Ingr.:

- 1 can (15 oz.) black beans, rinsed and drained
- 1 ripe mango, peeled and diced
- 1 avocado, peeled and diced
- 1/2 red bell pepper, diced
- 1/4 cup red onion, finely chopped
- 2 Tbls cilantro, chopped
- 2 Tbls lime juice
- Salt and pepper to taste

Proc.:

1. In a bowl, combine black beans, mango, avocado, bell pepper, and red onion.

2. Add cilantro and lime juice, season with salt and pepper.

3. Gently toss to combine all ingredients. Serve chilled or at room temperature.

N.V.: Calories: 225, Fat: 7g, Carbs: 36g, Protein: 8g, Sugar: 15g

Quinoa Salad with Lemon-Tahini Dressing

P.T.: 15 min.

C.T.: 15 min.

M. of C.: Boiling

Serves: 4

Ingr.:

- 1 cup quinoa, rinsed
- 2 cups water
- 1/2 cup cherry tomatoes, halved
- 1/2 cup cucumber, diced
- 1/4 cup red onion, finely chopped
- 2 Tbls tahini
- 2 Tbls lemon juice
- 1 garlic clove, minced
- Salt and pepper to taste

Proc.:

1. Cook quinoa in water according to package instructions. Let cool.

2. In a large bowl, combine cooled quinoa, cherry tomatoes, cucumber, and red onion.

3. Whisk together tahini, lemon juice, garlic, salt, and pepper to make the dressing.

4. Pour dressing over the salad and toss to coat evenly.

N.V.: Calories: 230, Fat: 8g, Carbs: 34g, Protein: 8g, Sugar: 3g

Spinach and Strawberry Salad with Poppy Seed Dressing

P.T.: 10 min.

C.T.: none.

M. of C.: No cook

Serves: 4

Ingr.:

- 4 cups baby spinach, washed and dried
- 1 cup strawberries, sliced
- 1/4 cup slivered almonds, toasted
- 2 Tbls poppy seeds
- 2 Tbls olive oil
- 1 Tbls apple cider vinegar
- 1 Tbls honey
- Salt and pepper to taste

Proc.:

1. In a large salad bowl, combine spinach, strawberries, and almonds.

2. In a small bowl, whisk together olive oil, apple cider vinegar, honey, poppy seeds, salt, and pepper to create the dressing.

3. Drizzle dressing over the salad and toss gently to combine.

N.V.: Calories: 180,

Fat: 12g, Carbs: 16g, Protein: 3g, Sugar: 10g

Chapter 9: Desserts and Sweet Treats

9.1 Fruit-Based Desserts for a Sweet Finish

Tropical Mango Tango Sorbet

P.T.: 15 min.

C.T.: none.

M. of C.: Freezing

Serves: 4

Ingr.:

- 3 ripe mangoes, peeled and cubed

- Juice of 2 limes

- 1/4 cup of honey

- 2 Tbls of fresh mint, finely chopped

- 1/2 cup of coconut water

Proc.:

1. Blend mangoes, lime juice, honey, and coconut water until smooth.

2. Stir in mint. Pour into a shallow baking dish.

3. Freeze for 4 hours, scraping every hour to fluff.

4. Serve chilled with mint garnish.

N.V.: Calories: 200,

Fat: 0.5g, Carbs: 50g, Protein: 2g, Sugar: 46g

Berry Bliss Frozen Yogurt

P.T.: 10 min.

C.T.: 4 hr. (Freezing Time)

M. of C.: Freezing

Serves: 4

Ingr.:

- 2 cups mixed berries (strawberries, blueberries, raspberries)

- 2 cups Greek yogurt, low-fat

- 1/4 cup agave syrup

- 1 tsp vanilla extract

Proc.:

1. Blend berries, yogurt, agave, and vanilla until smooth.

2. Pour mixture into a freezer-safe container.

3. Freeze for 4 hours, stirring occasionally.

4. Serve with fresh berries on top.

N.V.: Calories: 150, Fat: 1g, Carbs: 28g, Protein: 8g, Sugar: 20g

Peach and Ginger Compote

P.T.: 10 min.

C.T.: 20 min.

M. of C.: Simmering

Serves: 4

Ingr.:

- 4 ripe peaches, sliced
- 1/4 cup honey
- 1 Tbls fresh ginger, minced
- Juice of 1 lemon
- 1/2 cup water

Proc.:

1. Combine all ingredients in a saucepan over medium heat.

2. Simmer until peaches are soft and the liquid is syrupy, about 20 minutes.

3. Let cool, then chill in the refrigerator.

4. Serve cold, garnished with mint if desired.

N.V.: Calories: 120,

Fat: 0.3g, Carbs: 31g, Protein: 2g, Sugar: 29g

Avocado Lime Popsicles

P.T.: 10 min.

C.T.: none. + Freezing Time

M. of C.: Freezing

Serves: 6

Ingr.:

- 2 ripe avocados
- Juice of 3 limes
- 1/3 cup maple syrup
- 1 cup coconut milk

Proc.:

1. Puree avocados, lime juice, maple syrup, and coconut milk until smooth.

2. Pour into popsicle molds.

3. Freeze until solid, at least 4 hours.

4. Run warm water over molds to release popsicles.

N.V.: Calories: 180,

Fat: 12g, Carbs: 20g, Protein: 2g, Sugar: 15g

Spiced Pear Crisp

P.T.: 15 min.

C.T.: 35 min.

M. of C.: Baking

Serves: 6

Ingr.:

- 4 ripe pears, cored and sliced
- 1 tsp ground cinnamon
- 1/2 tsp ground nutmeg
- 1/4 cup almond flour
- 1/4 cup rolled oats
- 2 Tbls coconut oil, melted
- 2 Tbls maple syrup

Proc.:

1. Preheat oven to 375°F (190°C). Toss pears with cinnamon and nutmeg.

2. Mix almond flour, oats, coconut oil, and maple syrup until crumbly.

3. Layer pears in a baking dish, top with crumble.

4. Bake until golden and bubbly, about 35 minutes.

N.V.: Calories: 180, Fat: 8g, Carbs: 27g, Protein: 3g, Sugar: 16g

Kiwi and Strawberry Layered Gelatin

P.T.: 15 min. + Chilling

C.T.: 5 min.

M. of C.: Chilling

Serves: 4

Ingr.:

- 2 cups kiwi, pureed

- 2 cups strawberries, pureed

- 4 Tbls honey (divided)

- 2 Tbls unflavored gelatin

- 1 cup water

Proc.:

1. Dissolve gelatin in water, then divide and mix half with kiwi and half with strawberry puree, adding 2 Tbls honey to each.

2. Layer kiwi and strawberry mixtures in glasses, chilling each layer before adding the next.

3. Refrigerate until set, about 4 hours.

4. Serve chilled with a dollop of whipped cream.

N.V.: Calories: 140, Fat: 0g, Carbs: 34g, Protein: 4g, Sugar: 30g

9.2 Low-Fat Baking: Cakes and Cookies

Almond Flour Lemon Cake

P.T.: 15 min.

C.T.: 30 min.

M. of C.: Baking

Serves: 8

Ingr.:

- 2 cups almond flour

- 1/2 tsp baking soda

- Pinch of salt

- Zest of 1 lemon

- 3 eggs

- 1/4 cup honey

- 1/4 cup unsweetened applesauce

- 1 tsp vanilla extract

Proc.:

1. Preheat oven to 350°F (175°C). Mix almond flour, baking soda, salt, and lemon zest.

2. Beat eggs, honey, applesauce, and vanilla. Combine with dry ingredients.

3. Pour into greased cake pan. Bake until golden.

4. Cool before serving.

N.V.: Calories: 230, Fat: 14g, Carbs: 20g, Protein: 8g, Sugar: 12g

Oatmeal Banana Cookies

P.T.: 10 min.

C.T.: 15 min.

M. of C.: Baking

Serves: 12

Ingr.:

- 2 ripe bananas, mashed
- 1 cup rolled oats
- 1/4 cup cranberries
- 1/4 cup chopped nuts
- 1 tsp cinnamon

Proc.:

1. Preheat oven to 350°F (175°C). Mix all ingredients in a bowl.
2. Spoon onto a baking sheet. Flatten slightly.
3. Bake until edges are golden.
4. Cool on a wire rack.

N.V.: Calories: 100, Fat: 3g, Carbs: 17g, Protein: 3g, Sugar: 6g

Chocolate Zucchini Bread

P.T.: 15 min.

C.T.: 50 min.

M. of C.: Baking

Serves: 10

Ingr.:

- 1 large zucchini, grated
- 1 1/2 cups whole wheat flour
- 1/2 cup unsweetened cocoa powder
- 1 tsp baking soda
- 1/2 tsp salt
- 1/3 cup honey
- 1/2 cup unsweetened applesauce
- 2 eggs
- 1 tsp vanilla extract

Proc.:

1. Preheat oven to 350°F (175°C). Mix flour, cocoa, baking soda, and salt.
2. Combine zucchini, honey, applesauce, eggs, and vanilla. Add to dry ingredients.
3. Pour into loaf pan. Bake until a toothpick comes out clean.
4. Cool before slicing.

N.V.: Calories: 180, Fat: 2g, Carbs: 35g, Protein: 5g, Sugar: 18g

Carrot Cake Muffins

P.T.: 20 min.

C.T.: 25 min.

M. of C.: Baking

Serves: 12

Ingr.:

- 1 1/2 cups whole wheat flour
- 1 tsp baking powder
- 1/2 tsp baking soda
- 1/4 tsp salt
- 1 tsp cinnamon
- 1/4 cup unsweetened applesauce
- 1/2 cup honey
- 2 eggs
- 1 tsp vanilla extract
- 1 1/2 cups grated carrots
- 1/2 cup raisins

Proc.:

1. Preheat oven to 350°F (175°C). Mix flour, baking powder, baking soda, salt, and cinnamon.

2. Beat applesauce, honey, eggs, and vanilla. Stir into dry ingredients with carrots and raisins.

3. Spoon into muffin cups. Bake until a toothpick comes out clean.

4. Cool on a wire rack.

N.V.: Calories: 150, Fat: 1g, Carbs: 32g, Protein: 4g, Sugar: 18g

Pumpkin Spice Cookies

P.T.: 10 min.

C.T.: 20 min.

M. of C.: Baking

Serves: 15

Ingr.:

- 2 cups whole wheat flour
- 1 tsp baking soda
- 1/2 tsp salt
- 2 tsp pumpkin pie spice
- 1 cup pumpkin puree
- 1/4 cup unsweetened applesauce
- 1/2 cup honey
- 1 egg
- 1 tsp vanilla extract

Proc.:

1. Preheat oven to 350°F (175°C). Mix flour, baking soda, salt, and pumpkin pie spice.

2. Combine pumpkin, applesauce, honey, egg, and vanilla. Add to dry ingredients.

3. Drop by spoonfuls onto a baking sheet. Bake until firm.

4. Cool on a wire rack.

N.V.: Calories: 110, Fat: 0.5g, Carbs: 24g, Protein: 3g, Sugar: 10g

9.3 Healthy Sweet Snack Alternatives

Cinnamon Apple Chips

P.T.: 10 min.

C.T.: 2 hr.

M. of C.: Baking

Serves: 4

Ingr.:

- 2 large apples, thinly sliced

- 2 tsp cinnamon

- 1 tsp granulated sweetener of choice (optional)

Proc.:

1. Preheat oven to 200°F (93°C). Arrange apple slices on a baking sheet lined with parchment paper.

2. Sprinkle with cinnamon and sweetener.

3. Bake until crisp, flipping halfway through.

4. Cool before serving.

N.V.: Calories: 95, Fat: 0g,

Carbs: 25g, Protein: 0.5g, Sugar: 19g

No-Bake Peanut Butter Energy Balls

P.T.: 15 min.

C.T.: none.

M. of C.: Chilling

Serves: 8

Ingr.:

- 1 cup oats

- 1/2 cup natural peanut butter

- 1/4 cup honey

- 1/4 cup mini dark chocolate chips

- 2 Tbls chia seeds

Proc.:

1. Mix all ingredients in a bowl until well combined.

2. Roll into balls and place on a baking sheet.

3. Chill in the refrigerator until firm.

4. Store in an airtight container in the fridge.

N.V.: Calories: 180,

Fat: 10g, Carbs: 20g, Protein: 5g, Sugar: 10g

Avocado Chocolate Mousse

P.T.: 10 min.

C.T.: none.

M. of C.: Blending

Serves: 4

Ingr.:

- 2 ripe avocados

- 1/4 cup cocoa powder

- 1/4 cup honey or maple syrup

- 1/2 tsp vanilla extract

- Pinch of salt

Proc.:

1. Blend all ingredients until smooth.

2. Chill in the refrigerator for 1 hour.

3. Serve with a sprinkle of sea salt on top.

N.V.: Calories: 240,

Fat: 15g, Carbs: 28g, Protein: 4g, Sugar: 17g

Coconut Date Bars

P.T.: 20 min.

C.T.: none.

M. of C.: Freezing

Serves: 8

Ingr.:

- 1 cup dates, pitted

- 1/2 cup almonds

- 1/2 cup shredded unsweetened coconut

- 1 Tbls coconut oil

- 1 tsp vanilla extract

Proc.:

1. Process dates, almonds, coconut, coconut oil, and vanilla in a food processor until sticky.

2. Press into a lined loaf pan.

3. Freeze until solid, then cut into bars.

4. Store in the fridge.

N.V.: Calories: 200, Fat: 10g, Carbs: 28g, Protein: 3g, Sugar: 24g

Zesty Lemon Quinoa Bars

P.T.: 15 min.

C.T.: none.

M. of C.: Chilling

Serves: 10

Ingr.:

- 1 cup cooked quinoa

- 1/2 cup almonds, chopped

- 1/4 cup lemon juice

- 1/4 cup honey

- 1/2 cup unsweetened shredded coconut

Proc.:

1. Mix all ingredients thoroughly in a bowl.

2. Press mixture into a lined square dish.

3. Chill in the refrigerator until set.

4. Cut into bars and serve.

N.V.: Calories: 150, Fat: 7g, Carbs: 20g, Protein: 4g, Sugar: 10g

Chapter 10: Beverages: Smoothies, Juices, and More

10.1 Detoxifying and Nutrient-Rich Juices

Green Detox Power Juice

P.T.: 10 min.

C.T.: none.

M. of C.: Juicing

Serves: 2

Ingr.:

- 2 cups spinach leaves

- 1 cucumber

- 2 green apples

- 1/2 inch ginger root

- Juice of 1 lemon

- 1 stalk of celery

Proc.:

1. Wash all produce thoroughly.

2. Cut fruits and vegetables to fit your juicer.

3. Juice all ingredients, starting with the greens.

4. Stir in lemon juice and serve immediately.

N.V.: Calories: 120,

Fat: 0.5g, Carbs: 30g, Protein: 2g, Sugar: 22g

Beetroot and Carrot Immunity Elixir

P.T.: 10 min.

C.T.: none.

M. of C.: Juicing

Serves: 2

Ingr.:

- 2 medium beetroots

- 4 large carrots

- 1/2 inch ginger root

- 1/2 lemon, peeled

Proc.:

1. Clean and peel the beetroots and carrots.

2. Juice all ingredients together.

3. Stir and serve immediately for best nutrient retention.

N.V.: Calories: 95,

Fat: 0.3g, Carbs: 22g, Protein: 2g, Sugar: 17g

Tropical Digestive Aid

P.T.: 10 min.

C.T.: none.

M. of C.: Juicing

Serves: 2

Ingr.:

- 1 cup pineapple chunks

- 1 mango, peeled and cubed

- 1/2 inch ginger root

- 1/2 lemon, peeled

- 1 small cucumber

Proc.:

1. Prepare fruits and ginger for juicing.

2. Juice all the ingredients together.

3. Stir well and serve immediately to enjoy its digestive benefits.

N.V.: Calories: 150, Fat: 0.5g, Carbs: 38g, Protein: 2g, Sugar: 34g

Antioxidant Berry Blast

P.T.: 10 min.

C.T.: none.

M. of C.: Juicing

Serves: 2

Ingr.:

- 1 cup blueberries

- 1 cup strawberries

- 1 cup raspberries

- 1/2 lemon, peeled

Proc.:

1. Rinse berries under cold water.

2. Juice all the ingredients together, berries first.

3. Serve the juice immediately to maximize the antioxidants.

N.V.: Calories: 90, Fat: 0.7g, Carbs: 21g, Protein: 2g, Sugar: 15g

Refreshing Watermelon Mint Juice

P.T.: 10 min.

C.T.: none.

M. of C.: Juicing

Serves: 2

Ingr.:

- 4 cups watermelon cubes

- 10 mint leaves

- 1/2 lime, peeled

Proc.:

1. Blend watermelon and mint leaves until smooth.

2. Strain through a fine mesh to remove pulp.

3. Stir in lime juice and serve chilled.

N.V.: Calories: 80, Fat: 0.2g, Carbs: 20g, Protein: 1g, Sugar: 18g

Cucumber Kiwi Quencher

P.T.: 10 min.

C.T.: none.

M. of C.: Juicing

Serves: 2

Ingr.:

- 2 large cucumbers

- 3 kiwis, peeled

- 1/2 lime, peeled

- A handful of fresh mint leaves

Proc.:

1. Juice cucumbers, kiwis, and mint leaves together.

2. Stir in lime juice for a refreshing twist.

3. Serve immediately to enjoy its hydrating benefits.

N.V.: Calories: 100,

Fat: 0.4g, Carbs: 24g, Protein: 3g,

Sugar: 20g

10.2 Smoothies for Digestive Health

Ginger Turmeric Digestive Smoothie

P.T.: 5 min.

C.T.: none.

M. of C.: Blending

Serves: 2

Ingr.:

- 1 banana
- 1/2 inch fresh ginger, peeled
- 1/2 inch fresh turmeric, peeled (or 1 tsp ground turmeric)
- 1 cup spinach leaves
- 1/2 cup coconut water
- 1 Tbls chia seeds
- Juice of 1/2 lemon

Proc.:

1. Blend all ingredients until smooth.
2. Serve immediately for best nutrient absorption.
3. Optional: Add ice for a chilled smoothie.

N.V.: Calories: 120, Fat: 2g,

Carbs: 25g, Protein: 3g, Sugar: 12g

Avocado & Mint Digestive Aid

P.T.: 5 min.

C.T.: none.

M. of C.: Blending

Serves: 2

Ingr.:

- 1 ripe avocado
- 1 cup spinach
- 10 mint leaves
- 1/2 cucumber
- 1 cup almond milk
- 1 Tbls honey

Proc.:

1. Combine all ingredients in a blender.
2. Blend until creamy and smooth.
3. Enjoy immediately to support digestion.

N.V.: Calories: 150, Fat: 8g

Carbs: 18g, Protein: 3g, Sugar: 10g

Pineapple Papaya Enzyme Booster

P.T.: 5 min.

C.T.: none.

M. of C.: Blending

Serves: 2

Ingr.:

- 1 cup pineapple chunks
- 1 cup papaya chunks
- 1/2 banana
- 1 cup coconut water
- 1 tsp flaxseed

Proc.:

1. Place all ingredients in a blender.
2. Blend until smooth and frothy.
3. Serve fresh for digestive enzymes boost.

N.V.: Calories: 130, Fat: 1g

Carbs: 30g, Protein: 2g, Sugar: 20g

Cooling Cucumber & Aloe Smoothie

P.T.: 5 min.

C.T.: none.

M. of C.: Blending

Serves: 2

Ingr.:

- 1 large cucumber, chopped
- 2 Tbls aloe vera gel
- 1/2 cup Greek yogurt, low-fat
- Juice of 1 lime
- 1 Tbls honey
- Mint leaves for garnish

Proc.:

1. Blend cucumber, aloe vera, yogurt, lime juice, and honey.

2. Pour into glasses and garnish with mint.

3. Drink immediately for a soothing effect.

N.V.: Calories: 100, Fat: 0.5g, Carbs: 22g, Protein: 4g, Sugar: 18g

Berry & Oats Digestive Smoothie

P.T.: 5 min.

C.T.: none.

M. of C.: Blending

Serves: 2

Ingr.:

- 1 cup mixed berries (strawberries, blueberries, raspberries)
- 1/4 cup rolled oats
- 1 cup almond milk
- 1 Tbls almond butter
- 1 tsp honey

Proc.:

1. Soak oats in almond milk for 5 minutes.

2. Add berries, almond butter, and honey to the blender.

3. Blend until smooth and creamy.

N.V.: Calories: 150, Fat: 4g, Carbs: 25g, Protein: 5g, Sugar: 15g

10.3 Herbal Teas and Warm Beverages

Soothing Ginger-Lemon Tea

P.T.: 5 min.

C.T.: 10 min.

M. of C.: Simmering

Serves: 2

Ingr.:

- 1 inch ginger root, thinly sliced
- 2 cups water
- Juice of 1/2 lemon
- 1 Tbls honey

Proc.:

1. Boil water and add ginger slices. Simmer for 10 minutes.

2. Remove from heat, add lemon juice, and stir in honey.

3. Strain into cups and serve warm.

N.V.: Calories: 40, Fat: 0g,

Carbs: 10g, Protein: 0g, Sugar: 9g

Chamomile Lavender Sleepy Tea

P.T.: 5 min.

C.T.: 5 min.

M. of C.: Steeping

Serves: 1

Ingr.:

- 1 Tbls chamomile flowers
- 1 tsp lavender buds
- 1 cup boiling water

Proc.:

1. Place chamomile and lavender in a teapot.

2. Pour boiling water over the herbs and steep for 5 minutes.

3. Strain into a cup and enjoy before bedtime.

N.V.: Calories: 0, Fat: 0g,

Carbs: 0g, Protein: 0g, Sugar: 0g

Turmeric Golden Milk

P.T.: 2 min.

C.T.: 8 min.

M. of C.: Simmering

Serves: 2

Ingr.:

- 2 cups almond milk
- 1 tsp turmeric powder
- 1/2 tsp cinnamon
- 1/4 tsp ginger powder
- 1 Tbls honey

Proc.:

1. Heat almond milk in a pot over medium heat.

2. Add turmeric, cinnamon, and ginger. Whisk well.

3. Simmer for 8 minutes. Remove from heat and stir in honey.

4. Serve warm in mugs.

N.V.: Calories: 60,

Fat: 2.5g, Carbs: 9g, Protein: 1g, Sugar: 8g

Warm Apple Cider Vinegar Drink

P.T.: 2 min.

C.T.: 3 min.

M. of C.: Mixing

Serves: 1

Ingr.:

- 1 cup warm water

- 2 Tbls apple cider vinegar

- 1 Tbls honey

- 1 tsp lemon juice

- A pinch of cayenne pepper

Proc.:

1. Warm water to a comfortable drinking temperature.

2. Mix in apple cider vinegar, honey, lemon juice, and cayenne pepper.

3. Stir well and drink warm.

N.V.: Calories: 50, Fat: 0g, Carbs: 14g, Protein: 0g, Sugar: 12g

Peppermint and Licorice Tea

P.T.: 5 min.

C.T.: 10 min.

M. of C.: Steeping

Serves: 2

Ingr.:

- 1 Tbls dried peppermint leaves

- 1/2 tsp licorice root, chopped

- 2 cups boiling water

Proc.:

1. Add peppermint and licorice to a teapot.

2. Pour boiling water over the herbs and steep for 10 minutes.

3. Strain into cups and serve. Can sweeten with honey if desired.

N.V.: Calories: 0, Fat: 0g, Carbs: 0g, Protein: 0g, Sugar: 0g

Chapter 11: 5-Week Meal Plan for Optimal Health

11.1 Week 1: Introduction to Your New Diet

DAY	BREAKFAST	LUNCH	DINNER	SNACK	DESSERT
1	Avocado Lime Breakfast Smoothie	Soothing Spinach and Avocado Salad	Herbed Lemon Garlic Chicken with Mediterranean Roasted Veggie Delight	Cucumber Boats with Hummus and Veggies	Almond Flour Lemon Cake
2	Greek Yogurt Parfait with Fresh Berries and Almonds	Ginger Carrot Ribbon Salad	Balsamic Glazed Beef Steak with Spicy Steamed Green Beans	Avocado Lime Chia Pudding	Berry Bliss Frozen Yogurt
3	Quinoa and Egg Breakfast Muffins	Fennel and Orange Digestive Delight	Citrus Herb Chicken with Lemon-Herb Steamed Broccoli	Quinoa Energy Balls	Peach and Ginger Compote
4	Protein-Packed Oatmeal with Chia Seeds	Minty Pea and Barley Salad	Spicy Paprika Chicken with Balsamic Roasted Brussels Sprouts	Spiced Roasted Chickpeas	Chocolate Zucchini Bread

5	Buckwheat Banana Pancakes	Beetroot and Goat Cheese Anti-Inflammatory Salad	Ginger Soy Tuna Steaks with Quinoa Tabbouleh with Fresh Herbs	Kale and Almond Pesto Dip with vegetables	Avocado Lime Popsicles
6	Savory Oatmeal with Poached Egg	Cooling Cucumber Mint Soup	Lemon Dill Cod with Farro Salad with Roasted Vegetables	Vegan Avocado Chocolate Mousse	Spiced Pear Crisp
7	Whole Grain Toast with Avocado and Radishes	Quinoa Tabbouleh with Lemon Dressing	Herb-Crusted Pork Tenderloin with Curried Roasted Carrots	No-Bake Peanut Butter Energy Balls	Kiwi and Strawberry Layered Gelatin

11.2 Week 2: Establishing Routine with Variety

DAY	BREAKFAST	LUNCH	DINNER	SNACK	DESSERT
1	Berry Protein Power Smoothie	Quinoa Tabbouleh with Lemon Dressing alongside Turmeric Ginger Chicken Broth	Walnut-Crusted Halibut with Lemon-Herb Steamed Broccoli	Spiced Roasted Chickpeas	Oatmeal Banana Cookies
2	Cinnamon Almond Milkshake	Fennel and Orange Digestive Delight with a side of Gentle Lentil and Spinach Soup	Basil Pesto Chicken paired with Mediterranean Roasted Veggie Delight	Cucumber Boats with Hummus and Veggies	Avocado Chocolate Mousse
3	Smoked Salmon and Avocado Toast	Soothing Spinach and Avocado Salad complemented by Zucchini Basil Velouté	Ginger Soy Tuna Steaks alongside Spicy Steamed Green Beans	Kale and Almond Pesto Dip with vegetables	Carrot Cake Muffins

4	Tropical Turmeric Cleanser Juice	Minty Pea and Barley Salad accompanied by Sweet Potato and Ginger Soup	Herbed Lemon Garlic Chicken with Quinoa Salad with Lemon-Tahini Dressing	Quinoa Energy Balls	Berry Bliss Frozen Yogurt
5	Quinoa Fruit Salad	Beetroot and Goat Cheese Anti-Inflammatory Salad with Healing Mushroom and Barley Soup	Balsamic Glazed Steak Rolls with Arugula and Pear Salad with Walnuts	Avocado Lime Chia Pudding	Peach and Ginger Compote
6	Greek Yogurt Parfait with Fresh Berries and Almonds	Ginger Carrot Ribbon Salad and Cooling Cucumber Mint Soup	Citrus Poached Salmon with Curried Roasted Carrots	Vegan Berry Sorbet	Chocolate Zucchini Bread
7	Buckwheat Banana Pancakes	Quinoa Tabbouleh with Lemon Dressing and Avocado Lime Chia Pudding	Lemon Herb Pork Chops with Balsamic Roasted Brussels Sprouts	No-Bake Peanut Butter Energy Balls	Kiwi and Strawberry Layered Gelatin

11.3 Week 3: Experimenting with Flavors and Textures

DAY	BREAKFAST	LUNCH	DINNER	SNACK	DESSERT
1	Green Detox Smoothie	Soothing Spinach and Avocado Salad + Ginger Turmeric Chicken Broth	Herbed Lemon Garlic Chicken + Mediterranean Roasted Veggie Delight	Cucumber Boats with Hummus and Veggies	Tropical Mango Tango Sorbet
2	Berry Protein Power Smoothie	Fennel and Orange Digestive Delight + Cooling Cucumber Mint Soup	Salmon with Avocado Salsa + Spicy Steamed Green Beans	Quinoa Energy Balls	Berry Bliss Frozen Yogurt
3	Avocado Lime Breakfast Smoothie	Ginger Carrot Ribbon Salad + Gentle Lentil and Spinach Soup	Quinoa and Black Bean Stuffed Peppers + Lemon-Herb Steamed Broccoli	Spiced Roasted Chickpeas	Peach and Ginger Compote
4	Quinoa and Egg Breakfast Muffins	Beetroot and Goat Cheese Anti-Inflammatory Salad + Zucchini Basil Velouté	Balsamic Glazed Beef Steak + Farro Salad with Roasted Vegetables	Avocado Lime Chia Pudding	Avocado Lime Popsicles

5	Greek Yogurt Parfait with Fresh Berries and Almonds	Quinoa Tabbouleh with Lemon Dressing + Sweet Potato and Ginger Soup	Ginger Soy Tuna Steaks + Buckwheat Risotto with Mushrooms	Kale and Almond Pesto Dip	Spiced Pear Crisp
6	Turkey and Spinach Breakfast Burritos	Minty Pea and Barley Salad + Healing Mushroom and Barley Soup	Herb-Crusted Pork Tenderloin + Balsamic Roasted Brussels Sprouts	Quinoa Salad with Lemon-Tahini Dressing	Kiwi and Strawberry Layered Gelatin
7	Buckwheat Banana Pancakes	Mediterranean Roasted Veggie Delight + Curried Roasted Carrots	Walnut-Crusted Halibut + Arugula and Pear Salad with Walnuts	Cucumber Boats with Hummus and Veggies	Almond Flour Lemon Cake

11.4 Week 4: Incorporating International Cuisine

DAY	BREAKFAST	LUNCH	DINNER	SNACK	DESSERT
1	Tropical Turmeric Cleanser Juice	Quinoa Tabbouleh with Lemon Dressing + Turmeric Ginger Chicken Broth	Tofu and Veggie Stir-Fry with Peanut Sauce + Mediterranean Roasted Veggie Delight	Spiced Roasted Chickpeas	Vegan Berry Sorbet
2	Buckwheat Banana Pancakes	Ginger Carrot Ribbon Salad + Healing Mushroom and Barley Soup	Chicken and Vegetable Stir-Fry + Spicy Steamed Green Beans	Cucumber Boats with Hummus and Veggies	Coconut Mango Rice Pudding
3	Protein-Packed Oatmeal with Chia Seeds	Fennel and Orange Digestive Delight + Zucchini Basil Velouté	Spicy Paprika Chicken + Lemon-Herb Steamed Broccoli	Kale and Almond Pesto Dip	Almond Butter Chocolate Chip Cookies
4	Quinoa Fruit Salad	Beetroot and Goat Cheese Anti-Inflammatory Salad + Sweet Potato and Ginger Soup	Spiced Pork Chops with Apple Chutney + Curried Roasted Carrots	Quinoa Salad with Lemon-Tahini Dressing	Vegan Avocado Chocolate Mousse

5	Whole Grain Toast with Avocado and Radishes	Soothing Spinach and Avocado Salad + Cooling Cucumber Mint Soup	Ginger Soy Tuna Steaks + Farro Salad with Roasted Vegetables	Avocado Lime Chia Pudding	Coconut Date Bars
6	Savory Oatmeal with Poached Egg	Minty Pea and Barley Salad + Gentle Lentil and Spinach Soup	Lemon Dill Cod + Buckwheat Risotto with Mushrooms	Cucumber Boats with Hummus and Veggies	Avocado Chocolate Mousse
7	Cottage Cheese and Peach Breakfast Bowl	Quinoa Tabbouleh with Fresh Herbs + Sweet Potato and Black Bean Chili	Walnut-Crusted Halibut + Arugula and Pear Salad with Walnuts	Quinoa Energy Balls	Peach and Ginger Compote

11.5 Week 5: Advanced Preparations and Batch Cooking

DAY	BREAKFAST	LUNCH	DINNER	SNACK	DESSERT
1	Cinnamon Almond Milkshake	Minty Pea and Barley Salad + Turmeric Ginger Chicken Broth	Herb-Crusted Pork Tenderloin + Quinoa Tabbouleh with Fresh Herbs	Spiced Roasted Chickpeas	Chocolate Zucchini Bread
2	Greek Yogurt Parfait with Fresh Berries and Almonds	Soothing Spinach and Avocado Salad + Cooling Cucumber Mint Soup	Balsamic Glazed Beef Steak + Mediterranean Roasted Veggie Delight	Avocado Lime Chia Pudding	Oatmeal Banana Cookies
3	Smoked Salmon and Avocado Toast	Ginger Carrot Ribbon Salad + Zucchini Basil Velouté	Lemon Herb Pork Chops + Lemon-Herb Steamed Broccoli	Kale and Almond Pesto Dip	Carrot Cake Muffins
4	Quinoa and Egg Breakfast Muffins	Beetroot and Goat Cheese Anti-Inflammatory Salad + Healing Mushroom and Barley Soup	Chicken Zucchini Boats + Balsamic Roasted Brussels Sprouts	Cucumber Boats with Hummus and Veggies	Pumpkin Spice Cookies

5	Protein-Packed Oatmeal with Chia Seeds	Quinoa Tabbouleh with Lemon Dressing + Gentle Lentil and Spinach Soup	Spicy Grilled Mackerel + Curried Roasted Carrots	Quinoa Salad with Lemon-Tahini Dressing	No-Bake Peanut Butter Energy Balls
6	Savory Oatmeal with Poached Egg	Fennel and Orange Digestive Delight + Sweet Potato and Ginger Soup	Garlic-Lime Lean Beef Skewers + Farro Salad with Roasted Vegetables	Cucumber Boats with Hummus and Veggies	Avocado Chocolate Mousse
7	Barley Breakfast Bowl with Mixed Berries	Mediterranean Roasted Veggie Delight + Sweet Potato and Black Bean Chili	Grilled Tilapia with Mango Salsa + Arugula and Pear Salad with Walnuts	Quinoa Energy Balls	Zesty Lemon Quinoa Bars

Made in United States
Troutdale, OR
06/05/2024